I0704386

Doctor Who: Episode-by-Episode

Volume 13 – Jodie Whittaker

(Unofficial and Unauthorised)

By Ray Dexter

A Spinderella Paperback

First published in Great Britain in 2022

This edition 2025

By Spinderella

1 2 3 4 5 6 7 8 9 10 11 12

A CIP catalogue record for this book is available from the British Library

ISBN: 9798365241749

Doctor Who: Episode-by-Episode

Volume 13 – Jodie Whittaker

(Unofficial and Unauthorised)

By Ray Dexter

For Aron and Maja, as always.

The first Doctor Who story Ray Dexter can remember watching is *The Ribos Operation*. His favourite story is *Inferno*. His favourite modern story is *Midnight*.

@ray_dexter

Thanks must go to: Andy 'Witchmark' Hunt, Jerome Jones, Sophie Derby, and Richard Saunders for their helpful comments.

Appreciation must go out to Andrew Pixley, David J Howe, Stephen James Walker, and Mark Stammers for their incredible work without whom no book on Doctor Who can be written.

Introduction

This is the latest of a series of books on watching Doctor Who. Why do we need another Doctor Who book? In simple terms it's because everybody watches it the wrong way. Ever since the widespread availability of video cassette recorders and their subsequently more advanced offspring, fans of the show have been able to watch Doctor Who whenever they want and in whatever order they want. In addition, since the 1966 story *The Savages*, when individual episode titles gave way to an umbrella title for a whole adventure, there has been an assumption that Doctor Who was a show about self-contained stories rather than an evolving narrative. The return of the show in 2005, with its re-introduced format of individual episodes was a clever return to the original premise of Doctor Who and frustrating for fans who want the proper title for a story, not something like *Hell Bent/Heaven Sent*. Under Steven Moffat the show has barely paid lip service to conventional structured stories and instead has carried through threads and plotlines through whole eras.

This series of books chronicle the show episode-by-episode. In so doing it allows the reader the opportunity to follow the developments of the character known as the Doctor in the order they were created and, in the process, highlighting some of the inconsistencies created by new teams taking on the job of making the show. If you are any kind of Doctor Who fan I do urge you to find the time one year[1] to watch your favourite

---

[1] That's funny, I started watching in 2012 and I finished in November 2015!

show, in order, from the start. The understanding and the deep love for the programme fostered will make it all worth it.

A note on watching Doctor Who

One of the frustrating things about being a Doctor Who fan is the 90 or so missing Episodes from the archive. As such, you cannot 'watch' Doctor Who from start to finish. There are gaps in the fossil record. Up until the late 1970s the BBC had a 'save video tape' policy and all episodes bar a few random examples kept for the archive were wiped to reuse the tape. This went on all the way through the Jon Pertwee era too. Fortunately, black, and white film copies for overseas export were made and many of these survived, but many episodes have been lost forever. Even more fortunately, from the beginning there had always been Doctor Who fans who recorded the audio soundtrack off the speaker on their televisions. This means that we can hear all the missing episodes – miraculous really. Another piece of luck was that a man called John Cura invented a technique called 'telesnaps,' where he would take small but good quality photographs of the episodes as they were broadcast on a television screen, giving interested parties a record of the show for a fee. He did a lot of work on Doctor Who, but not every episode was 'telesnapped.' Since the 1980s when these telesnaps were rediscovered fans have been marrying the tape's soundtracks (now beautifully restored and with linking narration, thanks to the BBC) to Cura's telesnaps to make slide-show versions of the missing episodes. They're not perfect but they are better than nothing. Many are available these days on the You Tube and have taken these reconstructions out of the hands of the underground fan scene. Some are very good indeed and the technology and dedication has come so far that some fans have created good versions of episodes where no telesnaps exist at all – a major problem during the final Hartnell stories, and any from after Cura's death in 1968. Technically the BBC could get annoyed with such copyright breaking reconstructions but, perhaps because of their guilt at the destruction of the episodes in first place, the painstaking work to put them together and the fact that they are non-profit making and done for love, they turn a blind eye. This dedication persuaded the BBC to animate some of the missing stories, to a degree of success. So, with the various media and access to You Tube you can now 'watch' every episode of Doctor Who.

None of this really affects you at this stage in the Doctor Who story. All the Thirteenth Doctor stories exist, and all Doctor Who stories have been released on DVD.

A word about the categories

Although Doctor Who can be thought of as episodic, each 'story' had its own assigned writers and directors and guest stars and as such it is convenient to block them this way. Each story therefore has its own categories. They are detailed below.

<u>Title</u>
At times this has been very easy, as for most of its life each story has a name on screen. It wasn't so easy for the Hartnell era where each episode had a title, and it became less easy when we got to 2005. I will go with convention where I can

<u>One line summary</u>
An attempt to give you a quick synopsis.

<u>Producer, Showrunner, Director, Writer</u>
The main creative team behind the show. Where they make their first appearance you will find a brief biography. In the modern era there are all sorts of executive producers and script editors. I will focus on the main players.

<u>Key Players</u>
Actors who play the significant characters in the show making their debuts. This can open up another can of worms, especially in this edition. For the purposes of this book, I am including the recurring actor who played the Master and the two voice artists who played K9.

<u>Anything else before we start?</u>
This section fills you in with some of the behind-the-scenes facts about the production.

<u>The Episodes</u>
This is the most free-form aspect of the book. It's anything that springs to mind as I watched the episode. Sometimes this takes the form of plot; this is especially true in missing episodes, where the subtleties of the story may not be known to the reader. In more well-known stories this may take the form of extended comments on how the story plays out and other things worth noting. Each episode starts with a briefly summary in italics from the *Radio Times'* listing blurb. Up to five asterisks will be by the Episode number giving my rating for the episode.

<u>Verdict</u>
This is my opinion of the story as watched in order.

<u>Other famous reviews</u>

Over the years there have been many books analysing and reviewing every *Doctor Who* story. Some were written by very famous *Doctor Who* fans, others by relative unknowns. This section is an attempt to provide a flavour of the opinions of the story and give the conventional view if it differs from my take on it. In the 21st century, with hindsight less of a thing, most of the reviews are from well-known fan web sites or newspaper reviews.

<u>Ratings</u>

The average viewing figures for the whole of the story. If any episode had a very high or very low rating this will also be noted. I have gone for the consolidated post catch-up online ratings as opposed to those on first viewing.

<u>Chart positions</u>

This is a less well-known set of data, but it is the current measure of new *Doctor Who*. This is the chart position for the story and, given the huge differences in audience figures between successful shows in the 1960s and now, it gives a better perspective to exactly how popular the show was in relation to other shows of the time. The figure in brackets takes the chart position this story received and rates it against other Doctor Who stories, thus providing a list of the highest charting Doctor Who stories (*Voyage of the Damned, Journey's End, The Next Doctor*) through to the lowest (*The Curse of Fenric* – which didn't appear to chart at all).

<u>Position in polls</u>

My position of the story in the Whittaker canon.

<u>What have we discovered?</u>

Again, anything new or anything pithy that can be said about the story is written here.

The story so far…on screen.

On the 22nd November 1963 two teachers from Coal Hill School, London (Ian and Barbara) go beyond the call of duty with regards to a strange pupil called Susan. She is a brilliant scientist and a sometimes-brilliant historian, but in other ways she shows huge ignorance. They follow her to a junk yard where they have an uncomfortable encounter with her cantankerous old Grandfather, who spirits them away in a police box significantly bigger on the inside than out. The old man is called the Doctor and he cannot control this box his granddaughter calls Tardis. They have a series of adventures, some set in the future, some set in Earth's past, some in 'sideways' worlds.

Early on, they encounter some vicious aliens called Daleks. After one particularly harrowing adventure in Earth's future, where our heroes over-turn a Dalek invasion of Earth almost single-handedly Susan leaves, having fallen in love with a member of the anti-Dalek resistance. Ian and Barbara continue to travel with the Doctor, becoming less angry at their abductor and more excited by the possibilities open to them to see the universe. However, after a particularly weird adventure on the Planet Vortis their enthusiasm wanes a little and after an adventure where the Daleks chase them through time and space, they take the opportunity to return to Earth in an abandoned Dalek time machine. The Doctor continues to travel with a variety of younger companions. We also discover another person from the same planet as him. In his last adventure the First Doctor, having been subjected to a variety of very draining procedures over the previous set of adventures, collapses, having been present at an attempt by metal creatures called Cybermen to drain the Earth of all its energy. As the credits close the old man's face turns into a much younger one.

This younger version of the Doctor was much more playful than the previous incarnation. He had an early obsession with hats and a lifelong obsession with his recorder. He soon met his most iconic companion Jamie, and they had a series of rather 'Earth in the future' style stories against a series of horrific monsters, the most famous being the Cybermen. Eventually, in an adventure where a race of people used thousands of Earth soldiers to fight wars the Doctor calls in his own people, the Time Lords to help out. He is put on trial, and it is revealed that he ran away from his people and stole the Tardis. He is found guilty, exiled to Earth, and given a new face.

The Third Doctor is a dashing, upper-class sort of character who simultaneously hates his exile on Earth, while paradoxically fitting in very well indeed. This version of the Doctor is happy to name-drop his own planet and its people suddenly, and the Time Lords become much more invasive in his life than before. In many ways this is a good thing, as Earth is subject to a vast number of invasions in this era. The Doctor hooks up with UNIT, which he met in his previous incarnation and becomes their Scientific Advisor, with an ever-changing laboratory that he can use to try and fix his Tardis. The 'UNIT family' as it was known become a regular feature of his adventures, and his muscle in times of trouble. During his time on Earth his arch-Time Lord nemesis, the Master returns to his life and carries out a series of convoluted plots to gain power. He also has trouble with reptile-like creatures who once lived on the planet, who believe the planet should rightfully be theirs.

The Doctor gradually gets more freedom to travel, but it is usually with the Time Lords' blessing, until Omega, a Time

Lord from the old times, a hero who died to provide the power the Time Lords live by, is found alive and well and going insane in an anti-matter world. The Time Lords, faced with a collapsing universe, summon the Doctor's previous two incarnations to help fight Omega. Their success leads to the Doctor getting his freedom to travel in his Tardis again.

A series of adventures follow where the Doctor fails to take his latest companion Jo Grant to Metebelis 3. This leads to the Third Doctor having a crisis of Buddhist contemplation upon meeting a giant spider on Metebelis 3 and virtually sacrificing his 'self' for the story.

The Doctor regenerates again into a very tall, eccentric, Bohemian man who gradually severs his connections with UNIT and yearns to travel the universe. He encounters a series of grizzly villains and the creator of the Daleks, Davros. His ability to show great anger and great charm makes him a formidable adversary. Initially he travels with Sarah Jane Smith but after he is called back to his home planet she is ditched on Earth. On Gallifrey the Doctor is accused of murdering the President but after a brutal battle in the Matrix, the collected knowledge bank of the Time Lords, the Doctor realises his true enemy is a horribly mutated Master. Surviving this the Doctor finds a savage as a companion and tries to teach her to be civilised.

After his adventures on Gallifrey the Doctor seems to feel he is untouchable and he embarks on a series of adventures where he jokes and quips his way through, barely drawing sweat. He even manages to find the six segments of the Key to Time, a device the Guardians of the Universe use to keep it in balance. After even the Black Guardian can't defeat him, he gets even more egotistical. With an equally know-it-all companion, fellow Time Lord Romana, and a know-it-all tin dog called K9 they become almost insufferable. Then, something happens…

We don't know what precisely as it's not seen on screen but the Doctor returns for a final series of adventures in a burgundy stylised uniform. The wise cracks and flippancy are gone. He has aged and seems weary. He starts to pick up a series of younger companions: Adric, Tegan, and Nyssa, the latter who discovers her father's body has been snatched by the Master in need of a new body. Finally, as the Master tries to run the universe by destroying Logopolis the Doctor falls to his death from a giant telescope.

The new incarnation is a much younger, vulnerable man. Here we have an incarnation that doubts his ability to solve problems. His companions don't help, being moany, whiney, and seeming to not really want to go on adventures. He seems exasperated by them. After an adventure against the Cybermen Adric sacrifices himself and dies. The Doctor seems haunted by this for the rest of his incarnation; in fact, his last words will be 'Adric.' The Black Guardian returns to get revenge and puts a treacherous companion Turlough onto the Tardis, who nearly succeeds in killing the Doctor. Again, the Guardian is thwarted, only for every foe the Doctor has encountered before to line up to attack him: Daleks, Silurians, Sea Devils, Omega: all beaten. There is even time for another Gallifrey plot which puts all five of his incarnations up against a fellow Time Lord's quest for immortality. Finally, on Androzani Major, with both him and new companion Peri dying from spectrox toxaemia he barely survives a brutal mud-spattered adventure. Peri is saved; but the Doctor is forced to regenerate. Up sits an arrogant, curly- haired man.

This new Doctor quotes Shakespeare and asserts his academic superiority on most of the universe, and Peri in particular, who seems terrified of him. To complement his brash personality this incarnation dons a horribly garish costume and marches around quite alien locales looking for trouble. Although rarely in trouble this Doctor is unfriendly but paradoxically seems to have more old friends in the universe than other Doctors – especially ones we haven't met before.

Precisely how long-lasting this incarnation was is difficult to be sure of as his timeline was interfered with horribly by the Time Lords, in particular one called the Valeyard. The Doctor was plucked out of time after a horrific adventure on Thoros Beta where (and again it's difficult to be certain) the Doctor behaved poorly, and Peri was killed to provide a body for slug-like creature called Kiv. Once plucked out of time the Doctor was put on trial for his continued meddling in the affairs of others, although ironically the trial itself was a farce designed to cover up the meddling of the Time Lords in Earth's history. The Valeyard turns out to be a future incarnation of the Doctor. Although the Doctor escapes this trial and has at least one other adventure – one we see through the prism of the Trial - he goes on to have a new companion called Mel, who he never actually meets but who he takes with him before he meets her – I know, I know. Finally, to add to the confusion an evil Timelord called the Rani pulls the Tardis out of time and the Doctor hits his head, which causes another regeneration...

The new Doctor is a quirkier more mysterious character, who claims to have secrets and has knowledge of the early machinations of the Time Lords. His adventures take on a more epic quality with huge monsters of universe-destroying nature being confronted and thwarted. After a few adventures he is joined by a character called Ace, who also has a mysterious back story. More sassy than previous companions the Doctor and Ace become a formidable partnership.

As far as on-screen adventures go, we don't know what happened to Ace and the Seventh Doctor as we only saw their adventures up until a story called *Survival*. There were at least 60 adventures chronicled in book form (Virgin New Adventures) and their canonicity is much questioned, especially when one story called *Human Nature* seemed to be repeated for the Tenth Doctor. After that, the only appearance was of an older Seventh Doctor involved with some shenanigans on the Dalek planet Skaro and removing the essence of the Master after a trial. Landing in contemporary San Francisco he is shot 'fatally' by a gang upon exiting his Tardis.

He regenerates into a Byron-esque long haired figure with a slight Scouse accent, who seems more human in his reactions to people, however we do not see enough on screen to draw definitive conclusions. Again, there are documented stories in book form, but they may not be definitive (especially as in one the Third Doctor regenerates early). At some point during this incarnation the Time Lords and the Daleks begin a Time War, and the Doctor is in the thick of it, causing him to regenerate again.

The Ninth version of the Doctor is a gangly man with a Manchester accent and who eschews the traditional dress of previous incarnations. We meet him possibly at the start of his life (although there is contradictory evidence to this) where he helps a young shop assistant escape the clutches of the Autons. The Doctor and Rose form a deep friendship and travel the universe together. This Doctor seems passive and wounded from the Time War and less likely to take centre stage. On their adventures they sometimes bring along Rose's boyfriend

Mickey and meet a very charismatic adventurer called Captain Jack Harkness. Just as we were getting used to this grumpy and slightly hesitant Doctor an encounter with the revitalised Daleks and their Emperor causes him to self-sacrifice and causes a regeneration.

The new Doctor is a cockney with a gregarious manner and a winning smile. He's a joker and a charmer and was therefore much easier for his companions to fall in love with, and with other people, including Madame Pompadour and a nurse at a boarding school at the start of the 20th century. He travels with enthusiasm and relish. He travels to alternate universes where the Cybermen were created on Earth and loses Rose to the self-same universe when The Daleks and Cybermen clash. His new companion Martha is even more in love with him than Rose was, although the feeling seems less mutual. A chance encounter with a Professor Yana on a planet called Utopia leads to the realisation that it is his old foe, the Master … and this leads to the Master winning big time on Earth and the Doctor reduced to a CGI creature. Only Martha's faith in the Doctor turns the world around.

The Doctor then travels with Donna, an older, more platonic companion. After an encounter with Davros, Donna is returned to a state with no memory, and he travels alone. As this Doctor travels more he becomes more arrogant and complacent, with no Time Lords or companions to restrain him. He deliberately messes with a fixed point in time and is warned his time is nearly up. It is with another Master plan which forces him to regenerate, despite him not 'wanting to go.'

The new Doctor is whacky, funny, unpredictable and his adventures take place in very time-screwy order. His companion is a girl he met when he first regenerated aged 10 who waited for him, she calls the Raggedy Doctor. Again, Amy has a huge crush on the Doctor which causes her to full on snog him. The Doctor counters this by adding Rory, her boyfriend and future husband to the crew. He also has many encounters with the enigmatic River Song, his wife, soul mate and as we find out, daughter of Amy and Rory. The universe is reset on several occasions.

The next Doctor is an older man with a Scottish accent. He has issues with his goodness and encounters The Master regenerated as a woman and calling herself Missy, who, like a lot of women in this era is funny, sassy, and flirty. Although not the only villain he meets, her presence is felt throughout the era. He ends up spending an unknown period of time as a professor at a Bristol university before a time slippage involving the Master, Missy and the Cybermen forced him to regenerate.

The story so far…off screen.

Remember that saying about a camel being a horse designed by a committee? The implication being of course that committees always make a mess of things. Doctor Who is the perfect riposte to this argument and shows that committees can produce brilliant work. In fact, it can be argued that Doctor Who's lasting success is entirely due to nobody owning the idea, nobody over-ruling others, simply a lot of hired hands doing a job. Andrew Pixley has unearthed documents that show that in 1962 the BBC commissioned a report on the feasibility of 'science fiction' programmes from two story editors, Donald Bull, and Alice Frick. Their conclusion seems to have been that little science fiction was good for television, as viewers preferred action adventures. A further report from Frick and another colleague John Braybon suggested science fiction books with good characterization, no bug-eyed monsters and low demand for special effects. Fast forward to March 26th, 1963, and Sydney Newman, a Canadian recently appointed as Head of Drama and Serials, held a meeting with Frick, Braybon, Donald Wilson (Head of Serials) and 'Bunny' Webber, (a BBC staff writer) to discuss a science fiction series to fill the early Saturday evening slot. A brainstorm seems to have given various ideas, including a space/time machine, scientific trouble shooters and the need for various identification characters, including a 'maturer man,' with some 'character twist.' Newman gave the maturer man the 'fled from his own world in a time machine' twist. Webber took these ideas and came up with a proposal he called *Doctor Who*. How all these ideas eventually made it to screen could take another book, but this is the essence of the matter.

The show was given to a young producer, Verity Lambert. She was Roedean and Sorbonne educated and became Sydney Newman's production assistant having been promoted from a typist's position. Described as 'full of piss and vinegar' by Newman she had never produced nor directed before, but with Newman's backing she was given the job, despite some rumblings from the more establishment figures at the BBC. She went on to produce some equally great shows including *Minder* and *Jonathan Creek*. Newman credits her as 'the one who realized it all' – as great a compliment as you can get. Lambert, along with experienced script writer David Whitaker created the show as we know it. She was responsible for casting William Hartnell as the Doctor.

All the great plans for education and no bug-eyed monsters fell apart though when the Daleks took off in a big way in the second story. Doctor Who's popularity continued to increase to a ratings peak of 13.5 million viewers with a story called *The Web Planet,* by which time a blueprint for the show had been established where stories would be either in the future, past or sideways. Writers known to be particularly skilled in one area or another were hired to write typical stories. Lambert left after two seasons and was replaced by a man called John Wiles. Wiles struggled to leave his mark on the show and argued terribly with Hartnell. Wiles resigned midway through Season Three to be replaced by Innes Lloyd. Hartnell's health was failing, and the ratings had sunk to an all-time low. Lance Parkin ascribes this fall to the success of *Batman* on ITV. Hartnell was replaced and Lloyd concluded that the only stories worth doing were ones with monsters. All he had to do now then cast a new person to play the Doctor. He managed it with aplomb, and Patrick Troughton continued in the role, playing a younger version of the same Doctor.

The new Doctor soon acquires his iconic companion Jamie, played by Frazer Hines. Innes Lloyd's other great innovation was to spend big money on a huge set and this type of *Who* adventure dominated the first two years of Troughton's reign. The type of story became known amongst fans as 'base-under-siege.' By Troughton's third season the wheels were falling off. None of the production team really wanted to be running the show and the stories become much more variable in tone and quality. This had an effect on the viewers and there was some discussion about whether the show had run its course. With colour television coming in and no extra money to make the show the idea of Earth-bound adventures in a 26-week series firmed up. Troughton wanted to leave too so Derrick Sherwin and Peter Bryant, reluctantly in charge at the time, cast Jon Pertwee and prepared to hand over the reins to someone who *did* want to be producer: a certain Barry Letts.

There followed a period of stability in Doctor Who. Dicks and Letts remained with the show for an unprecedented (up to then) five years, as did Jon Pertwee. The show shook off some of its starchy, futuristic Earth-in-crisis appearance of the first season and became a more matey reflection of Letts' world view and his religious beliefs. Buddhism and spiritual ideas became very popular indeed and the ratings soared. The show embraced colour and a new effects technique called Colour Separation Overlay (green screen), which at its best allowed lots of great effects, but at its worse was used to save money on sets. After five years the show was on a high when Pertwee, Letts and Dicks all felt it was time to move on…

The new production team were Philip Hinchcliffe and Robert Holmes. Together they were absolutely determined to produce the best Doctor Who they could. They managed it. For three years they made gripping television, admittedly the roots were showing. We got *Frankenstein*, shape shifters, and other B-movie rip offs, but it worked so well. The horror was cranked up and this would be their undoing. One horror shot too many though caused Hinchcliffe to be moved to another project and humour being pushed instead.

The new producer was Graham Williams. He had many problems: inflation meant the money wouldn't go as far, *Star Wars* was raising the bar, and Tom Baker was proving increasingly difficult to manage, ad libbing like crazy. His script editor was Anthony Read, a classicist who liked to add Greek Mythology to stories and the umbrella concept of the Key to Time was a welcome innovation. By Season 17 came along Douglas Adams was script editor and the silliness was starting to overwhelm.

Williams resigned when he couldn't stand Baker anymore and in came the Production Manager John Nathan-

Turner. He created a whole new feel to the show. New theme, new titles, new costume. And within a year, a new lead actor too. The Nathan-Turner era was a new (and perhaps false) dawn; the early stories had a modern, ethereal quality never seen before, but this early promise soon disappeared as reviving monsters proved extremely popular to an increasingly vocal hard-core fan base, who the producer listened to increasingly. His script editor was Eric Saward, a man who liked macho stories about mercenaries and the show pushed a violent, confusing agenda with gaudy guest stars, returning monsters and over-lit sets. The returning Robert Holmes penned the last story of the Davison era and pushed the envelope as far as it would go, or so we thought.

Summarising the messy behind the scenes politics of the Colin Baker era is an impossible job, suffice to say that all the problems that had been brewing for years came to a head and the show was cancelled by the controller of BBC television, Michael Grade. A huge protest, led by the Producer gave it a temporary reprieve and the show came back for a limp 14-episode second chance. By then neither the Producer nor the Script editor wanted to be there but could find no escape route. The planned *Trial of a Time Lord* season was marred by the death of Robert Holmes and an increasingly upset Saward, who resigned before the season was completed and refused to let the team use his material. The final episode was written in a hurry by Pip and Jane Baker and Colin Baker was fired. As we leave the Colin Baker era the show has never been less popular or more likely to die.

The Sylvester McCoy era doesn't start too well with a jaded producer who wanted to be elsewhere and a new script editor with limited experience, but over the three years that they had they somehow managed more often than not produce some sublime television. Inspired by comic book storylines and reimaginings the Seventh Doctor was more mysterious and more powerful than previous ones. Knowing more and fighting bigger enemies. A lot of the current Doctor mythology was formed here and was the basis for the iconic Virgin New Adventures novels. The show was put up against Coronation Street and the ratings were disastrous. After three years, the powers that be, learning from what happening before quietly side-lined the show rather than cancelling it, leading to nearly ten-years of no Doctor Who on the television.

In 2004 the BBC want top writer and huge Who fan Russell T Davies to work for the BBC and the first show he wants to make is Doctor Who. They can't say no and Doctor Who comes back as a season of thirteen 45-minute episodes, with great CGI and a Christmas special. This new iteration of Doctor Who is a tremendous success. The first choice of Doctor, Christopher Ecclestone leaves after one season and there has been no definitive reason for why. It could have been for good reasons, or perhaps very bad reasons. The next choice, David Tennant was much more in tune with Doctor Who lore, being a huge fan himself and he relished his time as the Doctor.

Moffat's appointment was wildly cheered by the fans, as his episodes had been universally acclaimed and was the natural choice. Unfortunately for Who fans another series he devised, *Sherlock* also became a huge hit, and his time was stretched. His era was synonymous with playing with the structure and the ideas of Doctor Who. What was a two-parter really about? Shall we kill the Doctor in the first part of the season and let it hang there for twelve months? Shall we have underlying themes throughout the season so that the idea of a story in the old sense is less clear? Although a hit with fans the general viewing public were less able to keep up with the show and it became more a cult show despite its popularity increasing at this time in the US.

Moffat was one of the most sought-after writers in the world and was also show-running the mega hit, *Sherlock*, which made a star of Benedict Cumberbatch. The pressure of running two shows took its toll on Moffat, and he probably stayed one season too long and struggled to find people who could write for the show without his input. The ratings did fall off and Moffat's last season had some of the lowest (in the UK) ratings in the history of the show.

Season 11 (New Era)

Title: The Woman Who Fell To Earth

One Line Summary: The Doctor's turned into a woman and nobody cares!!!

Showrunner: Chris Chibnall

Adopted as a child and born in Liverpool he studied Drama at St Mary's College, Twickenham and did an MA in Theatre at Sheffield University. A Doctor Who fan since he was a child, he got into tv writing after a stint working on football stats at Sky Sports. His first series credit was *Born and Bred* for the BBC. This led to writing an episode for the classic *Life On Mars* and this led to writing episodes such as *42* for Doctor Who. He was lead writer on the Who Spin-off *Torchwood*.

His most famous series is the crime drama *Broadchurch*, set in Dorset, where he currently lives. It starred Jodie Whittaker as Beth.

He doesn't like the term 'Showrunner,' as it implies it's all down to him and it is, in fact a team effort.

Producer: Matt Strevens

He also worked on *Born and Bred,* but also *Skins, Misfits,* and the biopic about the making of *Doctor Who: An Adventure in Time and Space.*

New Cast: Jodie Whittaker

Yorkshire born and trained at the Guildhall school for Drama in London. she went into theatre early in her career. She really came to prominence the Chris Chibnall-written drama *Broadchurch*. She described her time on Doctor Who as the best fun she had on a job ever.

Bradley Walsh: Born in 1960 Walsh is a variety tv stalwart and the well-known face of hit tv game show *The Chase*. He is one of the most recognisable faces in Britain. He had done some acting work before, including *Coronation Street* and *Law and Order*, on which Chibnall was the executive producer. Chibnall described him as a 'gorgeous screen actor': but it was not the thing for which he was most known. Walsh was invited to lunch and told it would be a 'long journey.' His family told him he had to do it. He is the oldest companion ever if you don't count Wilf and um Romana.

Tosin Cole:

Born in New York City but moved to the UK when his parents separated. He got into acting at 16 when he joined an after-school theatre group and when he was taken to see a play called *Sucker Punch* starring Daniel Kaluuya. It was life-changing because he saw people acting 'who looked like (him).' Had a small part in *Star Wars: The Force Awakens* and was a regular in an *Eastenders* spin off show called *E20*.

Mandip Gill

Born in Leeds and studied acting at UCLan in Preston. She starred in Channel 4 soap *Hollyoaks* for a few years. Before then and down on her luck she had drawn a cheque for £5000 in her notebook and done some Cosmic Ordering and parts started coming her way.

Written by: Chris Chibnall

Directed by: Jamie Childs

He started his directing career by winning a competition to shoot a TV commercial for Patricia Cornwell's latest novel at the time, *Book of the Dead*. His winning piece was shown on Channel 5. Known for his short films and promos he was the one who directed the reveal of Whittaker as the Doctor. After Doctor Who he moved on to the BBC adaptation of *His Dark Materials*.

Music: Segun Akinola

After initially learning the piano and drums at an early age, he later turned his attention to composition, graduating from the Royal Birmingham Conservatoire with first-class honours and the National Film and Television School with an MA in Composing for Film and Television. He was a rising star Brit winner in 2017 before getting the Doctor Who gig.

Anything else before we start?

One of the problems with documenting the Whittaker era is the secrecy. Chris Chibnall keeps his cards close to his chest, unlike the less discrete Davies, who published his diaries, and we knew of all the problems, and a whistle blower who went to satirical magazine *Private Eye* to talk about production problems during Moffat's era. We don't know what Chibnall thinks about many things, he doesn't do social media and it's doubtful whether there will ever be a Chibnall diary release. Therefore, a lot of what was going on is kept under strictest secrecy and it may be years before we know what was really going on. What we do have are snippets from interviews. A typical Chibnall preview (and this could apply to almost any episode is: 'there will be thrills and spills, laughter and tears.')

On Whittaker: "Firstly, she's one of the greatest actors of her generation. But I thought – and I'd been guilty of this – the parts she'd taken didn't necessarily demonstrate her energy and physicality, her humour and her clownlike qualities."

In her audition, he recalls, she "brought the Doctor in with her straightaway." Her idea for the Doctor fused Christopher Lloyd as Doc Brown in *Back to the Future* with Madonna in a trouser suit. "Having spent most of *Broadchurch* sobbing on screen, she pleaded: "Can I please not cry?" Chibnall says, "I promised her she wouldn't be crying for a long time."

Chibnall claims that in writing for her he leaned into a childlike quality shared by actor and character – "like she's in a cave and the lights come on, at every moment," – plus a pragmatism and love of engineering and science that have inspired young female fans.

It might also be helpful at this stage to see how Chibnall describes the writing process under his watch. The key description for how he sees Doctor Who was recounted by Joy Wilkinson, who will write *The Witchfinders* later in this season. Doctor Who was "sci fi structured like a thriller, written like a comedy, with the texture of horror." And designed for intelligent 8-year-olds. Now, this might explain a lot about what we are going to watch, and it was clearly a mantra, as the other new writers on the show hint at similar direction.

So, Chibnall arrives at a script with these things in mind. He has the basic idea and write but the characters wrestle the story from him.

In terms of story lines Chibnall had a big document with ideas and stories and 'we ended up doing all of them.' He instigated a writers' room, a very US tv idea, where the chosen writers throw ideas around and are assigned scripts to work on.

The title here is presumed to be about the Doctor and the opening shot suggests that too but there is a chance it refers to Graham's wife Grace (note the name) and the themes related to her.

Chibnall said before the start of the next season (12) that the plan for season 11 was: "I think in the first series we had a really specific intent, which was ten single episodes which would demonstrate the sort of range and breadth of Doctor Who. Lots of different stories and anybody could drop in any week, and that was very deliberate."

Chibnall watched this at Madison Square Gardens in NYC, as it went out live in front of 5000 people.

"It would not be my preferred place to watch something that I've written with other people because I quite like to hide away. But it was incredible actually. I couldn't avoid being there because we were at New York Comic Con. And it was an amazing event."

The Episode

It starts off with Ryan talking on YouTube about the greatest woman he ever met and seeing him struggling to ride a bike with Bradley Walsh as his granddad Graham. His dyspraxia is a 'thing' in this first season, although it is hardly touched on in the second season, except for his final scene. After the throwing the bike over the edge of the hill in frustration a weird series of predictable science fiction cliches happen to him.

Yaz is shown as a probationary police officer wanting more and she gets it with Ryan's giant blue onion cliché in the forest. So far so obvious. There is nothing wrong with any of this so far.

Graham and Grace are in a convenient old train (with doors you should be able to open but can't) when it halts, the lights go out and the strangely empty train stops. And it stops, we're told, between Hathersage and Grindleford, which is fine, but that means the train is heading TOWARDS Sheffield, so what city is that in hills we see? (Clue - it's Sheffield). Why are they on a train going to Sheffield when they were already in Sheffield (and yes it must be Sheffield because Yaz is a 'fed' in

Sheffield) and then Yaz arrives very quickly? Look I've even done the Google maps. They're 29 minutes away from Sheffield.

A tentacle approaches them, then the Doctor falls into the carriage. It must be the longest the Doctor has not been on the screen since the very first episode. The Doctor does that thing new Doctors do now and does comedy pockets and is shocked by being a woman. Half an hour ago she was Capaldi. And isn't it a coincidence that the new incarnation has the local accent? Is that always true? The 'fam' get together to investigate what happened because this is how drama works.

A couple of ne'er do wells kidnap the onion thing and are watching it. No explanation is given for why. The onion splits open, with predictable dry ice. The tentaclely thing arrives on a roof.

"Where's my sister?" asked the man guarding the onion. But he is murdered quickly by another alien in human form. The alien steals a tooth. I'll tell you now, I didn't see that coming. No-one saw that coming.

An attempt to show the fam interacting and being normal is partially successful as the Doctor suddenly collapses in a post regeneration coma. She wakes up and says they have DNA bombs attached to collarbones. This is a pointless injection of pseudoscience peril that isn't peril because, well who believes it?

The Doctor stays at a slightly wacky pitch and figures things out, oh and forges a new sonic. We're in Sheffield, you see. Yaz finds some (very convenient) clues and the timing makes no sense. Then we get the first depiction of a comedy drunk for a while as a guy throws kebab salad at our humanoid alien. Comedy drunks are always welcome.

The Doctor finally meets the alien that has a name like Tim Shaw and, let's say, he's a badly nuanced alien: just badly thought through. "One touch of my cold skin will kill a human," is a typical line. Rubbish.

One thing that is good is the slightly scrappy, faded industrial setting; Doctor Who hasn't done that before. The other problem is that this is the Doctor doing stuff wackily and being the centre of attention and the many companions stand around saying the odd line of dialogue, just because they're on the payroll. We'll see this a lot.

Various shenanigans on a building site (which is quite a lot of crane action) and you get the feeling that this is not amounting to much.

Whittaker says the sort of Doctorish things you want Doctors to say. Tim Shaw kills off Grace because that's drama, right. And we realise at the start that Ryan is talking about his Nan, not the Doctor.

Ryan tries to cycle again, but why go into uneven hilly hills to try?

The Doctor, days later, is still wearing Capaldi's clothes. There's a well-executed charity shop clothes rummage bit, some technobabble to find the Tardis and, oh, the fam have all been transported too.

A story which is an alien is sent to randomly kill a human and is thwarted quite easily isn't exactly ground-breaking or particularly interesting.

Verdict:

In 1986 new show runner Chris Chibnall (aged 16) appeared on a tv programme called *Open Air* to review the 23rd season of Doctor Who. Famously, he seemed unhappy with the state of the show, suggesting it was a bit clichéd, could have been better written and featuring silly monsters. Now I'm not necessarily a believer in karma but if you then choose to become a tv scriptwriter and you end up as the Showrunner on the very same show, at the very least you've drawn a line in the sand about how your version will be judged by others.

Unlike many Who fans, I'm a fan of Chris Chibnall; *Broadchurch* was simply great, and his alternative take on the *Great Train Robbery* (2012) was equally good. We'll skirt over his Doctor Who and *Torchwood* work at this stage, just to be fair and judge this as a new era. You see, Chibnall always had a problem with taking this job on. He is a HUGE fan, and he knows all the stuff about the show that we do. He may have his tv writer's hat on and pretends to be cool and above mere fandom, but he knows the score, despite his almost blasé attitude he has given in interviews. He is one of us.

Modern Doctor Who writing has itself become a cliché. Always difficult to pigeonhole it's hard for potential science fiction and fantasy writers to get the show, despite it being seen as a SF/fantasy show – because it **isn't** pure science fiction or fantasy. The most successful Who writers have either had a background in comedy (Terry Nation, Douglas Adams, Steven Moffat – and with a slight stretch – Bob Baker and Dave Martin), or jobbers who just want the work (Robert Holmes). As neither followed the established rules of sci fi and Doctor Who (or even knew there were rules) they warped ideas because nobody knew the rules. All the producer had to do was take a great actor and get them to say the lines and away you go. The problem with the last seven-years is that they have cemented a style on Doctor Who that was never there before. Partly this is because it is the norm now for writers new to the series to claim (and lie) that they have 'always' been a massive Doctor Who fan and writing what they think Doctor Who is, and partly this is because the showrunner has one idea about what cool Doctor Who is. This 'scene that celebrates itself' has turned the once eccentric little British show into a huge worldwide behemoth, with its own set of clichés. This is a bad thing and Chibnall is right to escape from it as fast as possible. So, he used nothing from the past at all (the inclusion of the Swiss army sonic was therefore a disappointment).

He will also know that first episodes are tough. Back in the day the first three introduction stories are all top-ten greatest ever episodes of Doctor Who. After that, well *Robot* worked…just; *Castrovalva* was barely ok and is two stories; *The Twin Dilemma* is possibly the worst ever; *Time and the Rani* – wait, scratch what I said about the *Twin Dilemma* – **this** is the worst ever; *Rose* was fine, as was *The Christmas Invasion. The Eleventh Hour* at the time was brilliant (until you realised that it was going to be the same for seven years!) and I can remember not one thing about *Deep Breath* except the steam punk feel. Chibnall knows all of this, and I wonder if therefore he went for a vanilla-like *Castrovalva* rather than a total reboot like *Spearhead From Space*. In fact, Chibnall cleverly ignores everything from the last seven-years and avoids jokes full stop.

The criticism hanging over the Moffat era was that he couldn't write nuanced women and there were arguments for both sides. My opinion wasn't that extreme. I think he struggled to write *any* characters without making them cool, funny nerds who could deliver a zinger line. So, everyone for seven-years was a cool, funny nerd and some of them happened to be women. I mean imagine if Moffat has written the first scene of a woman Doctor – there would have been a breasts joke, or two, actually three. Chibnall is right to start again but he could have gone further and should have just had the Doctor turning up fully regenerated. Chibnall knows what is needed, but could he escape completely? Of course, the jury is still out. This is a team here acutely aware of the Bechdel test.

Yes, Chibnall starts again, and the first episode echoes that very first episode, *An Unearthly Child*: certainly, the crew is set up that way, and getting the companions home seems to be the driver. Old hands like me look at Bradley Walsh and remember Bernard Cribbins and you know there is a league of difference between the two.

Aside from that there isn't much wrong with what's on screen, it just isn't particularly impactful. It looks great, but there is a problem, and it is that my 13-year-old niece (a girl who has not watched Doctor Who since David Tennant) commented that it felt it should have been on CBBC. And she was right, it was played for children, and this is echoed in the publicity material. It must be said that Doctor Who has never been made for children. Its whole shtick has been that it was an adult's programme that children loved to watch (that was secretly actually made for children). This reboot is tonally confused, and the teenagers thought it was childish.

Yet Whittaker shines from her first scene and has won over many doubters out there. Chibnall is clever enough to recognise that you can't just write a generic Doctor Who story, it must be crafted to a female and whether they go there in the 'me too' world will be interesting.

Similarly, as Chibnall suggests, I recommend watching Whittaker with the sound down. She is so expressive, so into the performance that you can tell exactly what she thinks just from her face. It is extraordinary.

The plot, if you can call it that, featured a baddie (we haven't had one of those for a while) with teeth for a face and some nasty weapons but it's flimsy stuff and it's a bit like the other monster in *Love & Monsters*. The characters Yaz, Graham and Ryan are all introduced; Yaz and Ryan are supposed to be teenagers but…are clearly not. So, you have the scene where a grown man is trying to learn to ride a bike on the Peak District hills and although it's all explained via the dyspraxia it seems a scene more suited to a person who is not old enough to drive rather than the actor playing the scene, who is in his late twenties. Also, the story lost all momentum as the Doctor recovered and the weird sister-stealing bit wasn't very well explained (another fan texted me to say he 'put the tea on' during these bits).

In the end it wasn't as good as it could have been and for someone who had at least a year to produce this, it's a little flat. Or put it this way: this is the 277th Doctor Who story to be aired since 1963. That's a heck of a lot of creative imagination and this story doesn't get close to making it into the top 200. I think the 16-year-old Chris Chibnall sitting on that old television talk show, loving Doctor Who and criticising Doctor Who and knowing in his heart what great Doctor Who is would be disappointed with that.

So, I will be watching again, but my thought as the end credits rolled over the new theme was – will the supporting cast keep up the Yorkshire accents for the rest of their time on the show?

Other famous reviews:

The minimalist approach is reflected in Akinola's version of the theme tune, which sticks heavily to the original but adds just enough to freshen it up. And that just about sums *The Woman Who Fell To Earth* up concisely. It doesn't reinvent the wheel. It's a refresh rather than a reboot and will hopefully serve to allay many of the more understandable reservations people have about so much change happening at once – Peter Dillon Trenchard – Den of Geek.

With so much heavy lifting to do, *The Woman Who Fell to Earth* felt surprisingly ... small – The Guardian.

It's not the total knock-out we all hoped it would be but *The Woman Who Fell to Earth* is a terrific palate cleanser and a real breath of fresh air for Doctor Who (it's not a cliché when it's true) – Patrick Sproul, Cultbox.

Ratings: 10.96 million (the highest rated premiere in the show's history). It was also the most watched show on UK tv that week, something that does not happen very often with Doctor Who.

Ranking: 18/24

What have we discovered? That changing the gender of the lead character isn't a big deal.

The Ghost Monument

One Line Summary: *Enlightenment* (the Doctor Who story) done in a *Mad Max* sort of way

Written by: Chris Chibnall

Directed by: Mark Tonderai

Tonderai's father wanted him to have a cast-iron career, so he went for architecture, but he says he was always more interested in stories. He was a Radio 1 DJ for a while in the 1990s, following John Peel's legendary show on the night shift before in his words, falling out of love with music.' He moved into radio production and eventually picked up a camera. By 2008 he was making acclaimed short films. He is now working solidly in UK drama, although the hackles of Who fans may be put up by his claim on his web page to 'have revamped the new Doctor Who.'

Anything else before we start?

Much of the pre-episode speculation was about a rogue picture put out by the BBC to tease the episode. 'Look who's with the Doctor!' screamed the post, with Whittaker at the front next to Bradley Walsh and a third male with a quiff obscured by sunlight. 'It's Captain Jack!' screamed the internet, when it was actually Shaun Dooley, one of the guest stars.

Dooley was also credited with taking one of the pictures the BBC used to publicise the series. He took it on his iPhone whilst on location.

For various reasons involving good deals and the wide variety of locations this was shot in South Africa, along with exterior shots in *Rosa*. They would repeat the experience for the next season. They rehearsed out there and there was a drought and Cole got heat stroke.

The Episode

It starts quite wobbly with Ryan clearly being earmarked as the character for the audience to empathise with: we're with him as he's waking up, Bradley Walsh has already done so. The pilot of the ship that scoops them out of space (Angstrom – because Swedish names are a thing in space[2]) has never heard of humans but clearly is one and speaks plot exposition to herself (just in case you don't know - this is bad writing).

The Doctor and Yaz are on another ship crashing and the Doctor solves the crash problem in a Doctory way, with more technobabble. It's not real and this is sadly going to be the way of the future. The ship crashes on an alien planet: and it's a beautiful and well realised shot.

Bradley Walsh and Ryan are there with their own alien (Sean Dooley). Occasionally Graham says something that is brilliant, like, when on an alien planet and not knowing where to go he just suggests following

---

[2] I'm well aware that they're aiming for the unit of measurement

the alien. That's what we want from Walsh and when his heart is in it, it's great.

As they walk through the alien landscape (South Africa looking convincingly other worldly) there is a scene the epitomises the new show. Bradley Walsh is moaning about the sand in his eye (man, you're on an alien planet experiencing things you can never imagine - stop moaning!) and the Doctor hands him some sunglasses she claims to have got from either Audrey Hepburn or Aristotle. Now, they were in the pocket of some clothes she got in a charity shop literally not that long ago. So, for practical purposes it's impossible. Or is she lying to show off? If she is, that's rubbish.

Anyway, then Bradley Walsh gives her the feed line: 'Aristotle didn't wear sunglasses,' and the Doctor says: 'You never saw him with a hangover.'

Now, I'm afraid it's not funny. The name-dropping Doctor character is fifty years out of date, and I don't think anyone should try funny Doctor Who – Steven Moffat killed that one dead. Go for contrast.

So far this is tired, or awkward, as if the creators are not fully onboard with the infinite possibilities of Doctor Who and are just doing cliché, yet Chibnall is familiar with Doctor Who.

We meet Art Malik as a hologram who explains the rules of the race, and this turns into something else. The Ghost Monument of the title turns out to be the Tardis, which nobody spotted. Bradley Walsh notes it is an old police box and Yaz says something like: 'Ooh, like the one on Surrey St but that's green.' Good local knowledge here. I checked, and it is green and looks absolutely nothing like the thing on the screen in front of Yaz, therefore even more impressive.

As noted, the characters in this story are aliens who have never heard of human beings or Earth. This is a great statement of intent, however there is no attempt to make them be alien by prosthetics, words, or actions. It jars. It would be better to have avoided it entirely. Russell T Davies was all about avoiding alienating the viewers, but this is going too far.

The Doctor practises Venusian aikido after fifty-years and it looks different to Pertwee. Sean Dooley's character is so inept you can't imagine 3998 people in the competition **not** as good as him if he's the best.

Bradley Walsh and Ryan pretend to fix a motor on a boat so they can have a scene together to discuss Grace. Then the Doctor tells them how to fix the engine because in the Doctor Who world of the 21st Century the Doctor can solve anything with a twirl of the sonic and a few words.

They rest as the boat goes across the sea and they find ruins. Gun slinging aliens meet them. Ryan has a Play Station moment so the Doctor can reiterate her 'no guns' policy and it works, although the tone is light (again).

The Doctor technobabbles about tunnels under half the planet. Then they recycle the plot of the *Enemy of the World* to have scientists working against their will.

Weird, scientifically designed killing machines that look like scarves try and kill them and call the Doctor the Timeless Child (we'll see a lot more of this). Some actual science related to acetylene is delivered and Ryan knows it's lighter than air from an NPQ, hmmmm. Which one?

The race is over, it's a draw, it's null and void, they all disappear. The Tardis reappears and it's quite a nice moment. Although the St John's Ambulance badge has gone, and the base is thicker.

Verdict:

Perhaps it's unfair to the new series but after 55-years nothing is new, and most things have been done before. But second episodes with a new Doctor and new backroom teams are quite rare and often more revealing than first episodes…

There haven't been many: The *Ark in Space, Doctor Who and the Silurians* and *The Beast Below*, and at times *The Ghost Monument* recalled all three of them. The Silurian tale is relevant but to a lesser extent. *Spearhead from Space had* already done a lot of the work for us regarding the new (3rd) Doctor but was produced by the old team and *The Silurians* was a reaffirmation that the Doctor wasn't going to be time travelling for a while. Yet the punchy power of the moral arguments on show in *The Silurians* really did get us to understand the new production team's ideas. *The Ghost Monument* had less to do in this regard, but it did reconfirm what we saw in the first episode: that the jokes are over, and this is going to feel more real.

Similarly, *The Beast Below* was a standard Steven Moffat in style and was typical of what was to come; with deliberate scary bits, a sassy female lead cracking jokes and a twist ending showing that nobody was a baddy (Good grief would we get sick of this). And although there is no hint of 'baddies' in *The Ghost Monument* at least we get ambivalence, selfishness, and some dark stuff in the background. Also cleared away was the awkward flirting and sexual confidence by EVERYONE. Time will tell if this is Chibnall's style but it's so refreshing to have a sexless show again.

If you *must* ape a second story, then *The Ark in Space* is the one you want to be like. It was a total reset of the Doctor Who universe. Gone was UNIT and in came body horror and an alien seriousness in tone. *The Ghost Monument* was trying something similar, to eradicate the past, so the prologue was removed completely (as clear a statement as you could get), as was the Doctor's easy familiarity with the universe. Here, the aliens have never heard of human beings and the Doctor had no clue about this world: extremely refreshing. This denial of the familiar is a brave step: Russell T Davies always argued that it's hard to emote with an alien and always wanted his characters to be humans being human (Davies took it further and had his future humans wear the same fashions as now). *The Ark in Space* as a comparison raises the bar but the start of *The Ghost Monument* sometimes felt that radical.

But there are echoes of other Doctor Who stories too, which some would argue was inevitable and refreshing, where, for others it's a warning sign. For really old school fans the flesh–eating bacteria in the water reminded us of the acid sea on Marinus but we didn't see it at work, so it was a little pointless. SHOW,

DON'T TELL CHRIS! *Enlightenment*'s space races are hinted at too, although we only see the end of the race and get no hint of the scale or the previous challenges. More obviously there were shades of *Marco Polo*, with a quest across a planet, with problems to solve, actual talking and finding out stuff. And for the first time is ages we, the audience, were finding out about the world at the same time, not deliberately being kept at arm's length. For too long our role has been to stand back and admire the finished product and the genius hand of the creator/showrunner and it got tedious. Here we feel like a companion. Now, let's be honest – this isn't a *Marco Polo* - like epic, as the story is set over two days not three-months, but if you're thinking like this it's not a bad idea.

What else was refreshing? There was a hint of solving problems with things that were lying around rather than sneaky time travel tricks and River Song doing something clever. For the first time in a long time, you didn't feel the hand of a producer on the shoulder who has decided that there is only one cool way for Doctor Who to be.

Although refreshing, this story didn't deliver quite enough. It sagged again at the wrong time. And although there were some good moments: Ryan's PlayStation moment – attacking the robots only for them to get up again thus vindicating the Doctor's 'no guns 'diktat – was great but the other companions are served less well (which has been the concern with three companions all along). Bradley Walsh plays Graham with an exasperated 'what's happening now?' mien but hasn't quite removed the look of 'I'm Bradley and I'm doing Doctor Who' from his countenance. And Yaz, well she just says some lines. Jodie Whittaker was spot on although it could be argued the Doctor gave up a bit easily at the end, and the perpetual moan of excessive sonic screwdriver use still gives us concerns that the money is spent on the visuals rather than the scripts.

There was no real underlying threat apart from hints at a bigger picture and no surprises, which either means they are leaving behind the portentous messages that the new series has lived on since 2005, or, if there *is* a bigger threat it's been hinted at very badly (*The Timeless Children*).

I hope I am wrong but to me it still feels very awkward now, like a film that recreates a time from the past you lived through, and they get the details wrong, so you keep pulling your attention off the narrative. It's as if we've reached that point where Doctor Who has been mis-remembered and misunderstood one iteration too far and has been put back together by archaeologists disguised as directors.

So, although there are promising signs, I'm concerned that they don't really know what they're doing and their idea of radical and my idea of radical are far apart.

Other famous reviews:

For all its flaws, *The Ghost Monument* screams 'confidence.' This is a show heading in a bold new direction with its best foot forward, and it's not afraid to take risks. Nothing exemplifies that more than the trailer for next week's episode – Den of Geek

It's another clearly told, linear adventure, realised with pace and panache, far sunnier than last week's *Torchwood*-lite grim-fest – Radio Times

This, on the other hand, is the Chibnall Who we were dreading. We know we hated Moffat's insistence that Who is a fairy tale, but nevertheless, done properly, it should have a sprinkle of magic about it. This, despite being on an alien planet, with actual aliens, is so utterly prosaic. It has about as much magic as an accounting seminar. Add to that plot and characters spelled out in letters of fire and an unacceptably wibbly Doctor, and we're just... Please tell us it isn't all going to be like this. – Androzani.com

Ratings: 9.0 million (3rd)

Ranking: 20/24

What have we discovered? There are parts of the universe the Doctor doesn't know, and no-one has heard of Earth. Enjoy it while it (briefly) lasts.

Rosa

One Line Summary: Doctor Who does *Quantum Leap*

Written by: Malorie Blackman, Chris Chibnall

A sixty-book veteran author, Blackman was Children's Laureate between 2013-2015 and most famous for her *Noughts and Crosses* series which uses a dystopic world to explore racism and it was made into a tv series in 2021. Before she became a full-time writer, she was an English teacher. She also wrote a short story called *The Ripple Effect* which starred the 7th Doctor and featured a universe of good Daleks and the Doctor's inability to accept that.

Directed by: Mark Tonderai

Anything else before we start?

Chibnall says that doing a story about Rosa Parks was in his initial pitch to the BBC. When he was offered the job, he said it was one of the things he wanted to do. It needed to be early on and it needed to be a statement of intent. At the first writers' room meeting Chibnall told the assembled talent that he wanted to do a Rosa Parks story. Pete McTighe remembers, "a beat of stunned silence in the room." As they were plotting it everyone was 'super excited at how new and different it felt." Blackman did an awful lot of research into Parks' life but was well aware that this was a Doctor Who story. At the press conference for Season 12 Chibnall admitted to sleepless nights over it and worried about getting it right. Even the fabric in Parks' costume is right for the clothes she wore.

This was also filmed in South Africa and took advantage of the deal outlined under *The Ghost Monument*. They were tremendously happy with how they managed to recreate 1950s America.

It is Bradley Walsh's favourite story by 'a country mile.'

The Episode

We start with an admittedly great looking, well-directed early scene with Rosa Parks on a bus, but not THAT incident. It will be true all the way through this era that modern Doctor Who makers have an inability to do good science fiction (if defined as 'specific otherness'). This is a real failing, but the historical, when done like this, shows a past that is more unfamiliar than any alien planet could be and still be a watchable mainstream show. There is a case that science fiction is now done as a genre, that our imaginations have reached a limit, that we cannot do alien anymore, whereas the past's appalling attitudes are fertile and more interesting. This sort of past is a good place to explore, especially in a political climate in the UK, which at the time seemed to fetishize the past as a glorious thing to be returned to and racism was on the rise.

The Tardis lands in Montgomery, Alabama in 1955 and you get an obvious Tardis interior bickering scene about the Doctor not being able to get them home. One of the strengths of Doctor Who is that it can tell any story, but one of its weaknesses is that it must keep doing these sort of scenes – make the companions want to go home. They did it quite well in Davison's era but when they could do it better in 1964, in one studio, you know there's a problem.

Artron energy is detected as an excuse to look round and Ryan immediately gets punched for touching a white woman. He then gets threatened with lynching. He takes it stoically, which is a response but perhaps not the one that's needed here. And Rosa Parks (of course) turned up to do some explaining and the fam are excruciating when they realise who she is. This is a profoundly serious subject, and this is a very pivotal character in the Civil Rights' Movement and this goofing around is not right. I can't imagine Malorie Blackman wrote this bit.

Ryan doesn't get served in bar and they realise that THAT bus protest is tomorrow. Once thrown out of the bar the tone is still too light for where we are.

At the bus station they find evidence of a time traveller whose motives are ambiguous. The Doctor gets some Doctorish moments, and they stay in a whites' only motel (when even Bradley Walsh points out that they could have stayed in the Tardis). The writing team try mild flirtation between Yaz and Ryan (bear that in mind later in this book).

We get a bank joke that was quite good. An encounter with a police officer that riffs on Steve Jobs and some nice detective work to monitor Parks. The scenes in the bus with the various ethnic zones is excellent, with minimal comedy. Vinette Robinson still seems to be in a different drama to everyone else, but everyone gets something to do, which is nice.

The Doctor confronts Krasko, the racist criminal from the future, who feels the universe isn't right because of Rosa Parks, which is a bit of stretch, but there we go. Ryan gets to meet Martin Luther King, at the time 'just' a pastor in the local church.

The Doctor notes that James Blake must drive the bus, but Krasko is making minor changes and he isn't going to be. The Doctor manipulates time to get the bus drivers back despite herself saying you shouldn't do it. Things get back to normal. Cole is very good in that naive style of his when he sorts out Krasko.

The climactic scenes on the bus where the crew can't help Parks are powerful.

"Stand up now."

"I don't think I should have to."

All ends 'well' but why we had to have the Doctor explaining everything at the end though worked. I think you could have left it with statements before the end credits.

Verdict:

This was broadcast in the UK on a day when a fat, vile old white man was filmed refusing to be seated next to an elderly black woman on a Ryan Air flight from Barcelona and using appalling language, would Doctor Who, confronting racism head-on for the first time, be part of the solution, or part of the problem?

Before seeing this episode two things concerned me:

1) that Doctor Who meeting Rosa Parks could go horribly wrong. Based on how the previous 13 years of Doctor Who had managed real historical characters, would Rosa Parks be turned into sassy, sexy woman who fancies at least two of the Tardis crew, one being female? Also, given the times we live in and important films like *BlacKKKlansman*, which are set in the past but are about the here and now, *Rosa* had a lot to live up to; getting the tone wrong would be an almost fatal blow to this new iteration.

2) I kept thinking about Douglas Adams. He famously concluded that almost nobody could write good Doctor Who. He made a real attempt to get new writers in when he was script editor and had given up by the end. With a new writer here, could she get to grips with Doctor Who?

It's so pleasing to have my doubts blown away. Mallory Blackman wrote a beautiful episode of Doctor Who that works so well you wonder why the previous regimes didn't try taking the past seriously too. Blackman is not a first timer of course, being the veteran of numerous children's books and a Doctor Who e-book.

Here of course, the bad guys are the racist white folk of Montgomery, Alabama and this pulls no punches in terms of the language used to describe Black people, or in the way life was if you were unfortunate enough to live there. It seems so unaccountably stupid to modern eyes when shown that the Black folk must stand at the back of the bus, or that 'coloureds' can't eat in some restaurants.

Yet it is heartbreakingly real and not exaggerated. Yaz's genuine confusion as to where she (with brown skin but not 'black') fitted into the segregation was well played, as it highlighted the pointlessness of it all. The whole set-up was shocking in a way that using aliens or going for allegorical racism on planet Zog (or the Ood) would have failed. This is in-your-face injustice, within living memory and it must be stopped, or in this case, the natural course of events must be allowed to happen.

Stylistically, there have been comparisons made to *Back to The Future* and *Quantum Leap* and both are fair; some have suggested this as a criticism (*The Daily Telegraph* really didn't like it): I don't see that. It works so well because it is ugly and brutal and not about aliens but is about evil in a way that people don't like to consider evil, the fact that a white man in a suit is the nastiest thing in the world. To quote Martin Luther King again: "Never forget that everything Hitler did in Germany was legal."[3] The token alien presence is handled well (remarkably) and dispensed with a light touch even if the motivations of someone from 7000 years in the future do seem a little stupid. It was as if Chibnall couldn't quite bring himself to do a pure historical, so the weakest of alien presences was added. A rogue time-traveller from 2019 would have made a lot more sense.

Whittaker gets it right big-time at last, she is clearly in charge – but not totally – but plays it a little too earnestly at times. Tosin Cole plays Ryan with a sad acceptance of the way things were and it works well

---

[3] Letter from Birmingham jail, 1963.

because of his dignity and lack of reaction. Bradley Walsh improves but there's still not enough to do for Yaz, despite Mandip Gill's best efforts: although the nice, if soapy scene with Ryan outside the hotel room as they describe racism in modern Britain was a good start.

On reflection this was the most surprising episode of Doctor Who since *Blink* and much needed, if just to break away from the stereotype of what a Doctor Who story can be. The direction by Mark Tonderai never felt forced and I felt I really was in Montgomery, Alabama. And the simple acceptance that we were here allowed us to have an educational treat, a direct comparison with now and an adventure where people can be heroic and dignified. This could have been a Hartnell historical.

Rosa is an important episode and the deliberate need by the Doctor to NOT interfere with history and allow Rosa Parks to be arrested is beautiful, because, as Martin Luther King said, "In the end, we will remember not the words of our enemies, but the silence of our friends" He could have been referring to the crew on the bus. It didn't put many feet wrong and sets a high bar for future Doctor Who. Have they finally banished the old style?

It has an ugly mood but the lightening of it with the smart phone line and Ryan's ignorance of what Rosa Parks was famous for were good at blurring the lines on how messy these things are in real life.

Other famous reviews:

Rosa is not a typical Doctor Who episode. The subject matter is heavy, the pace is slower than usual – to allow the full horror of the setting to sink in – and the sci-fi elements are sorely lacking. But as a one-off it's a powerful piece of drama, and one which is sure to have families talking to one another about it long after the end credits have rolled - Den of Geek.

The actual plot, however, is as rickety as a ladder in a hurricane. – The Independent.

A well-intended but poorly executed riff off history – Daily Telegraph.

Ratings: 8.41 million (4th)

Ranking: 5/24

What have we discovered? You can do historicals without them being whacky (enjoy it while it briefly lasts).

Arachnids in the UK

One Line Summary: City of the Spiders and Donald Trump is ripe for satire.

Written by: Chris Chibnall

Directed by: Sallie Aprahamian

Vintage director with three decades of TV work, going back to the iconic *This Life* in the 1990s and prior to that, theatre work.

Anything else before we start?

Chibnall had to accept the plot similarities to the 2002 comedy horror film *Eight Legged Freaks*. In Doctor Who terms the obvious nod would be to the 1974 Pertwee swansong *Planet of the Spiders* but you'd be looking in the wrong place because this environmental take is much more like the previous season's *The Green Death*. Chibnall asserted that Doctor Who had "only flirted with spiders a few times but never really done a story entirely focussed on them." – Hmmm.

The title was Vinay Patel's courtesy of the Writer's Room –and plays on the title of the punk band, the Sex Pistols' first single *Anarchy in the UK*.

It was filmed in Sheffield and Wales. The hotel is Celtic Manor golf course and resort near Newport. The tower blocks are Park Hill in Sheffield.

Getting Chris Noth was a bonus, as the part of Robertson was written generically but once casting director Andy Prior mentioned the name it became irresistible.

The spider science is all based on facts and Dr Niall Horan, an Australian conservationist and spider expert was consulted to get it right. Tanya Fear, playing spider expert Dr Jade McIntyre wasn't a fan of spiders.

The Episode

That Mr Big from *Sex and the City* does his Donald Trump impression in a Sheffield hotel and in the process of establishing his bad guy corporate credentials fires Yaz's mum, although we don't know that it's Yaz's mum yet.

The Tardis lands in Sheffield. Job done Fam; off you go…you'd think. Bradley Walsh goes home and sees a ghost. The Doctor goes for tea at Yaz's. Yaz's mum, as we know, has been fired by Donald Trump and the Doctor goes to pick up a parcel from a flat two doors down but there is no answer to a knock.

A person called Jade is also looking at the mysterious flat. They break in. The flat is suitably webby. "Lot of cobwebs for a few days," says Ryan. Anna, the owner is covered in cobwebs and is dead. And the reveal of the monster spider, when it comes, is fabulous. Spiders hate the smell of garlic. Who knew? It looks great. And

Jade turns out to be a spider expert (coincidence) and in his gaff Bradley Walsh has also found a huge spider.

Spiders attack people and Yaz goes to pick up her mum at the 'well swanky' hotel. Donald Trump has cobwebs in his rooms and blames Yaz's mum. At the university, the Doctor name drops Amelia Earhardt. That's a line: 'there's something wrong with the spider ecosystem of South Yorkshire.'

The Doctor does some scribbling and works out where the epicentre is – oh, it's Donald Trump's hotel. Yaz and her mum also encounter massive spiders.

Donald Trump does the stereotypical bathroom germaphobe thing and an enormous spider comes out of the bath. The bit where he leaves his bodyguard to die is glorious.

Everyone teams up to solve the problem but there's a scene when they all come down an escalator and you realise, you're watching a drama with seven people all in the same place, all needing something to do. If you're counting: the Doctor, three companions, the owner of the hotel, Yaz's mum, who's there because she knows the building and a spider geek. It's too much. There follows a scene in the kitchen where Robertson is grilled, and everyone has a good line. But like in *Rosa*, it's the wrong tone. Again, to whom is this pitched?

Graham and Ryan catch a spider and are chased by the CG beasties. We're told the hotel is built on a waste disposal site. Toxic waste is making the spiders huge. *Green Death* vibes old skool Who fans. Loud, modern music attracts all the spiders. Did they research this? (Apparently so). It's Stormzy with *Know Me From*.

Yaz's mum is used as a way of checking on the relationships between Yaz the Doctor and Ryan. Yaz looks confused by any relationship, remember that.

The big spider is dying and too big to breathe. The Donald Trump clone kills her and doesn't care.

The fam go back in the Tardis and have more adventures.

Verdict:

Immediate responses to Doctor Who stories have changed over the years. When I was at school the critical response was done on the school bus the following day and was polarised down the middle between the fans, who always loved it, and the non-fans who always took the time to laugh at it (except of course after *Earthshock* episode 4, which was just universally agreed to be epic). Having just written that sentence I realise that the world hasn't moved on much, as social media still works the same way. Erstwhile producer John Nathan-Turner was famously quoted as saying that "The memory cheats," when remembering old stories; this was in response to hard-core fans berating him for producing Doctor Who they didn't think was good enough. Yet I remember watching Part 1 of *The Trial of a Timelord* and thinking it was brilliant, yet now I am less enamoured. We're extremely poor judges of quality in the moment. So, JN-T was right (and wrong), but the 'memory cheats' argument should be less persuasive in an era when we can watch most Doctor Who episodes any time we like. We can make comparisons instantly. So, as I scrolled through Twitter after *Arachnids in the UK,* I was amazed at how many responses were like 'this was the best, scariest Doctor Who story ever.' Now, it clearly isn't. No matter what you think of Steven Moffat's era of the show it was hard-wired to try and find things to you to fear and this did none of those things quite as well. And 'best' is such a strong word when it just **can't** be the best episode ever. What I'm trying to say is that trying to get an objective opinion on a story in the immediate aftermath is almost impossible, so (foolishly) this is my attempt to do just that.

There's something very right about the season being based in Sheffield. It gives an immediate fresh perspective, and the time vortex looks totally gorgeous. And if you are going to do 'scary' then giant spiders are the way forward. The CGI rendered spider's first appearance was extremely impressive and the way that everyone on screen was unhappy with the idea of huge spiders was great. We got none of the 'wow, isn't it gorgeous' we might have got under Russell T Davies. The director has seen *The Shining* and uses Kubrick's style well; the writer has researched spiders diligently and uses everything in the script. The plot itself, in which a hotel mogul with morals not unlike the current (at the time) President of the United States (even down to the germophobic flourishes) was a bit obvious and a throwaway line that he wasn't Trump and hated him and was going to run against him in 2020 wasn't enough to get over the stupidity of this. That he has built a luxury hotel on a festering landfill site brought this viewer straight back to the 1970s and this felt like a mash up between *The Green Death* and of course *Planet of The Spiders.*

So, despite minor misgivings, for 40-minutes you had a beautifully rendered piece of television. The constant fear that the large crew will struggle to have things to do was kicked down the road for another week as Yaz's family were introduced, giving her some lines. This gave us our convenient 'in' into the plot while Ryan and Graham got on with the spider capturing. The biggest problem here was that science geek Dr Jade McIntyre totally owned the episode, knowing all about spiders and getting a few good lines. She made Yaz a little redundant, especially as her police background has hardly been touched on and here, we had a guest star who could help the Doctor. Get her in the Tardis!

What was strange was the resolve, the spiders were lured via Stormzy, and ~~President Trump~~ Robertson shot the big spider that was dying anyway. No moral, just the bad guys won. And the Doctor wasn't even annoyed; she just took off for more adventures. At the time I felt I'd missed something and rewatched it to check, but that was it. For the first time I questioned whether Whittaker has got the characterisation right. She spent a lot of time being kooky and enthusiastic but just let this wrong go unpunished. That's not right. It's not for me to tell an actor where to look but watch any Matt Smith episode and you can see how it can be done. We needed another scene with

Chris Noth as ~~Trump~~ Robertson chewing scenery and getting on with his life, or another scene where the Doctor deals with the wrong and Robertson (think of the last scenes of *Family of Blood*).

This ended up being a very flawed episode of Doctor Who that riffed off old stories but didn't do them as well (its failure reminded me of *The Hungry Earth/Cold Blood* – another misguided Chibnall attempt at re-doing the Pertwee era). Chibnall has a very understated approach to Doctor Who, but at the moment there is not a clear direction of travel because of it: it's just episodes of Doctor Who. I appreciate that is what he is trying to do, but the current crew, as they stand cannot help him. Ian Chesterton used to be fists, arguing with the Doctor and science; Barbara Wright was History and moral core; Susan was screams, weird space stuff, tripping over and eye candy. I know this is simplistic but none of the current crew have any special talents or ways into the story. We just don't have classic identification figures with useful skills, they just do things when the script demands it. The series will suffer until they find a better direction and a proper sense of what all the characters can do.

And the Doctor can't let people get away with things like this and she seems to. See *Kerblam!* For more weird Doctor behaviour when confronted with extreme capitalism.

Other famous reviews:

"These spiders are a dream!" – Radio Times

If *Rosa* was made more powerful by its refusal to rely on allegory, *Arachnids* stumbles for precisely the same reasons. Robertson isn't merely evocative of Donald Trump – he namechecks Trump, he disdains Trump, he wants to *be* Trump. The last time a president was cited in Doctor Who it was the tongue-in-cheek reference that Obama was going to unveil a plan to single-handedly save the world economy, and even that drew some ire for being clumsily partisan. I'm not certain there's any deeper meaning for Robertson here beyond "Donald Trump is BAD, guys," but whatever your political point of view, this half-baked caricature is not exactly insightful commentary -Den of Geek.

It's not all terrible. As usual, Bradley Walsh kills the grieving husband bit, and his and Ryan's relationship gets another nice boost. Where she's allowed to be, which is hardly ever, Jodie is terrific (we particularly love her "I call people "dude" now!"). Yaz is always a pleasure to spend time with, although the RTD-era family stuff added little, unless you think giant hints that she might not be straight are massively shocking character development – Androzani.com.

Ratings: 8.22 million (4th)

Ranking: 11/24

What have we discovered? It's pretty but vacant (geddit).

The Tsuranga Conundrum

One Line Summary: Male pregnancy and teeth-pulling terribleness

Written by: Chris Chibnall

Directed by: Jennifer Perrott

Australian who came to prominence with a film called *The Ravens* in 2016. Before that she directed episodes of *Hollyoaks* and *Home and Away*. She has also directed episodes of *Gentleman Jack*. Strangely it is credited as Directed by… rather than Director. Is it significant? Time will tell.

Anything else before we start?

The P'ting was named by Tim Price, who is a writer and participated in the writers' room but never got a screen credit. Not sure this is compensation. However, uniquely, he does get a credit for creating the P'ting. Sounds like an obscure Doctor Who pub quiz question.

This is another story where there were clearly problems in pre-production. Some suggest that it was at script level, with a lot of telling but not showing. Others wonder whether the cryptic way the Director is credited 'Directed by' instead of Director suggests something. One day the omerta will go and we will find out.

The Episode

On a junk planet Bradley Walsh finds a sonic mine that the Doctor can't stop from exploding because the plot requires it to blow up. Remember kids, in a future episode a similar peril will be able to be stopped by the sonic. That's modern sophisticated science fiction writing for you.

They regain consciousness in a space hospital. The Doctor wants to leave to get the Tardis back. They meet someone who is apparently famous (Eve Cicero), and the Doctor tells them (for us): "You helped defeat the army of the aeons at the battle of the Underkite," which is an attempt to do a Robert Holmes and paint worlds with words. It nearly works. And, although the Doctor's 'I'm a huge fan schtick is embarrassing at least she does the same thing to other famous people (like Rosa Parks), so it's consistent weirdness.

And then there's a pregnant male, because it's time there was one, but it's for comic effect. Chibnall has talked about how being adopted made him question where he was from and the scene where the pregnant man talks of giving away the baby must have been very hard to write.

Something breeches the ship for a second. I can see why this looked good - on paper but it's realised so badly that it's childish. Is it the writing, the direction, the tone? The something mentioned above is a P'ting. It's a grumpy CGI monster. We're told it can survive in a vacuum and doesn't need to breathe, but it has a nose. It eats the Doctor's sonic. They can devour all organic material.

The action moves to a 'stop the ship being destroyed by the planet they're trying to get to and/or the P'ting by protecting the antimatter power system.' The Doctor works out the P'ting feasts on energy, which is fine, but all organisms do that, but they also need proteins and minerals. It's too simplistic. Energy won't make minerals.

The general does some piloting. The Doctor finds the self-destruct bomb and is going to give it to the P'ting. It all resolves (like it wasn't going to) without any hint at tension.

Ok and let's address the male pregnancy thing. Yes, yes, it's the future but if you're not going to …um explain how and why, it's just plain stupid and it's not something a throwaway line can solve. It reeks of inclusivity (And that dreaded attempt to be PC) but it's so badly done as to be embarrassing. Tokenism is worse.

And then the biggest problem - the Tardis is abandoned on a junk planet, and we don't see how they get it back.

Verdict:

There has been some criticism of this episode online and to be honest it's not difficult to see why. Even the staunchest fans of the new series would have to admit that the four Chibnall-penned episodes have all been slightly underpowered; that they didn't quite go far enough and that perhaps they were a bit rubbish. Now I should admit something at this point; I am currently re-watching a lot of Matt Smith era Doctor Who for another project and I had just watched *The Impossible Astronaut* before watching *The Tsuranga Conundrum*. It's an unfair comparison of course but *The Impossible Astronaut* must be one of the best episodes of new Doctor Who (in fact any Doctor Who) in terms of design, alien threat, punchy dialogue, and confidence. This, tragically, is one of the worst.

If we consider Chibnall's two previous Doctor Who space stories set on spaceships we see a recurring pattern. *42* was a good (if obvious) idea of a countdown threat that received mixed reviews from fans. *Dinosaurs on a Spaceship* was also poorly received but was saved by impressive performances from Smith and David Bradley. The dinosaurs themselves and the excruciating robots were not helpful. Here again, *The Tsuranga Conundrum* was a series of obvious space story clichés produced via a series of missteps. The real fear is that our showrunner can't write science fiction set in space, which might be a deal breaker for a series like Doctor Who.

The opening section on an alien rubbish dump and a sonic mine threat is perfectly acceptable, if a little unexplained and then leaps to a hospital ship on a course to the nearest safe planet. At this point the Doctor still seems to be injured but this is purely for effect and is soon ignored. The other patients are introduced: a pregnant male (that seems so obvious for a production team that cast the Doctor as a woman as to surely have been rejected at the drawing board stage) there to bring light relief. This is a story that does not need light relief. It is also there to give Graham and Ryan something to do – deliver the baby.

The 'Space pilot' Eve Cicero, her engineer brother, Durkas, and android Ronan have uses for the plot, but are hardly better drawn. The Doctor and the chronically underused Yaz (again) have their own problems with the P'ting, the energy devouring alien that is threatening to eat the ship and is toxic to hold. On paper that sounds fantastic but the realisation of the P'ting is frankly terrible. It's cute, cartoonish and poses no threat. Even the devouring of the sonic screwdriver destruction is reversed.

In the end the monster is used to devour the self-destruct mechanism and is booted out, the space pilot and her engineer brother pilot the ship to safety. The android does nothing, Ryan and Graham deliver the baby and Ryan won't take the fist pump from Graham (oh I can't wait for the final episode when Ryan **does** allow Graham to fist pump him). And then it's all over.

This never went beyond a cartoony run around some nice corridors. An energy-eating impossible-to-kill alien eating the ship from around them is a genuinely great idea but the way it was done here was just completely wrong. Moving away from Moffatian story arcs and cleverness was needed but this isn't the way forward. This feels too childish rather than for children. It certainly isn't cool and without cool it can't go on for long.

On Twitter some clever wag put up a picture of notoriously verbose, classic poorly received Doctor Who writers Pip and Jane Baker with the caption 'Just for fun! You are Pip and Jane Baker! Give Chris Chibnall some advice!' Another wit posted Chibnall's own comments on that infamous programme with Pip and Jane where Chibnall is quoted about their story *Terror of the Vervoids*. Chibnall described it as "very clichéd, very routine…running down corridors…silly monsters…not very challenging to watch...the story has been done on different ways over the last few years…" If only he could have seen the future! And just in case you're not getting it, remember *Terror of the Vervoids* was a story set on a spaceship, with a threat of imminent destruction, lots of corridors and a ludicrous alien threat. The criticism will hurt Chibnall, and it is undeserved, but he didn't have to write such a clichéd story, and in his wildest dreams he never imagined he'd write a story less well-received than a Pip and Jane Baker one!

Five episodes of evidence in and it is hard to see any explanation other than the current team have no idea how to make Doctor Who anymore. But we live in hope: there's always next week…

Other famous reviews:

With a scant ten entries this year, five of which are now said and done, filler episodes might not be good enough to convince sceptics that the show is able to mesh its rediscovered human factor with the grander narrative themes of yesteryear. – Den of Geek

Not so much flawless as without any major issues, at several points veering into fascinating but still basically uninspiring, and an all-around good showing for the period. – Elizabeth Sandifer – Tardis Eruditorium

Optimism destroyed once again, can only put their faith in things looking up once Chibnall isn't hogging all the scriptwriting – Androzani.com

Ratings: 7.76 million (6th)

Ranking: 22/24

What have we discovered? No matter that you think you've seen the worst Doctor Who story is there's always capacity to make one that's worse.

Demons of the Punjab

One Line Summary: The One with the misdirectional title.

Written by: Vinay Patel

Born in 1986 he is known for plays such as *An Adventure, True Brits,* and *Free Fall.* His television debut, *Murdered By My Father,* a powerful drama about honour killing, won the 2016 Royal Television Society Award for Best Single Drama and was nominated for three BAFTAs.
 Patel said: "I grew up watching shows *like Star Trek* and *Quantum Leap* on the edge of my dad's bed, and I loved how they managed to capture the imagination of a kid like me as well as acting as a moral compass. I never imagined that I'd get to write for Doctor Who – I was pretty thrilled."

Directed by: Jamie Childs

Anything else before we start?

The new writers were recruited under a cloak of secrecy, not even being told which show they were working on. When it was all revealed Patel, Peter McTighe and Joy Wilkinson all agreed that the lunch they went to when they met was very intimidating, especially for Patel, who didn't have an on-screen television credit at the time. They were given a CD of songs that were 'the embryonic vibe' of what Chibnall was envisaging. They were also asked to put on a 'post it' note what the essence of the show was. They went for 'the Doctor travels in time' but Chibnall reversed it and said it was all about the companions.

Two weeks later they started the story rooms where a lot of the ideas for many of the stories over the next two seasons came from. Patel was very green about Doctor Who and writing and was in awe of his other writers. Patel said to himself, "If I only had one shot to tell story through Doctor Who what would it be?" and the partition of India was top of the list. Given the sensitive subject matter Patel insisted that nothing he invented could be worse than the real violence of the time. The aliens must be thematic to the story (The Thijarians are his grandparent's names backwards) and the Doctor could not save the day.

"A lot of drafts of scripts have got 'he' in. The writers didn't know – nobody knew – until that reveal video went out." However, Chibnall said he doesn't feel that the deception changed the content of the stories much, with the new Doctor's gender (or rather, the Doctor's new gender) rarely impacting on adventures any more than it did when s was at the he was played by male actors.

"It's very hard for me to think of a decision that the Doctor has taken in 55-years that is a gender-based decision or action," Chibnall explained.

"I'd really struggle to think of one."

Except, of course, when the Doctor enters historical time periods which may have a slightly less advanced view of gender politics…

"I think particularly in the historicals – *if* we're doing historicals, which I'm sure we are – obviously, that then affects what happens to all these characters when you go to certain periods of history," Chibnall allowed.

The screenwriter went on to pay tribute to his group of Doctor Who writers, who are all new to the series and whose announcement brought great excitement earlier this summer.

"I was looking for…great writers!" Chibnall said. "It was the next generation of writers for Doctor Who in terms of people who can come in and own the show, and having writers from diverse backgrounds was really important to me, as well.

"With writers it's like actors – you read their work and you respond to their work. All of them absolutely adore the show, all of them have been banging down the door to get an opportunity, so it's just people who had stories to tell and understood what we wanted to do with this iteration of the show."

The scenes in India were filmed in Spain, specifically Granada.

The theme of remembrance was deliberate because they knew it would be broadcast on Remembrance Sunday.

The Episode

This starts beautifully with Yaz's grandma giving away gifts including a watch in flashback and Yaz is hassling the Doctor to go back to Pakistan in the 1950s. They land in scenery that to my untutored eyes looks right (even though it's actually Spain). They hitch a ride, and the Doctor has a weird experience that tells us some sci fi is happening. They find out it's actually 1947 and the partition of India is happening.

But there are also demons standing over a holy man. Chasing the demons, who the Doctor has never encountered before they realise the aliens accompany the alone when they die. Got that?

We meet Yaz's grandma (like we weren't going to). The usual quibbles like Yaz's Nan has a different accent in 1947, see *Blink* for another example.

The Doctor here is cracking too many jokes and at inappropriate times. We can accept this is the 13th Doctor's persona, but it's unfortunate, especially in historicals. You can see we're getting the drama of two people in love from different sides.

The Doctor's statement about the black stuff in the jar is the densest organic matter is quite simply the biggest pile of scientific nonsense I've heard in a long time.

The Thijarians aren't assassins, and the Doctor apologises for thinking they were demons. However, as ever with a time travelling alien - why not? - there would be no present or future. Prem, Yaz's grandma's Hindu love interest dies today at the hands of his radicalised brother, and the companions out vote the Doctor to stay. Bad move but good drama.

The thugs arrive after the wedding the watch gets smashed, and history plays out. Yaz's mum has put her hand on a map and decides on Sheffield. "Such an exotic name."

The end scenes are simply great, and the alien bits at the death make it when it really, really shouldn't.

But the overriding reality is that historical stories have a limit: they are either 'we can't change history, not one line' (which as discussed ad nauseum, is stupid because this rule never applies to contemporary or futuristic stories), or it's simply set in the past for an interesting backdrop and involves minor adventure peril. Here, it was a bit of both.

Verdict:

It's episode 6 and is there starting to be a theme? We'll get there in a bit – the clue is in the title – but let's look at the piece in general first.

I remember 30-years ago thinking that one way to save the show would be to do a whole series of historical adventures. The theme could change and be played on a harpsichord. You could find people who could write interesting stories and weren't put off by science fiction and still have an interesting show. There are probably very bad reasons for this idea but in some ways, this is the first series for 50 years to attempt genuine historicals and the old fans, like me, are always going to love it. The historicals are certainly saving the day this season.

Demons of the Punjab is set on August 1947, the day that India was partitioned by the British creating Muslim Pakistan and non-Muslim India (this is a huge simplification). The violent consequences and uprooting of literally millions of people is a blot on the historical map and the consequences still rumble today. Writer

Vinay Patel had the problem that his story needs to be small scale to fit into the budget and 50-minutes, so as the Doctor reluctantly yields to Yaz's request to investigate her grandmother's history they aren't taken to Lahore, Pakistan as expected, but the land where the border is about to be drawn. Using radio broadcasts skilfully the viewer gets the background picture quickly and we get to focus instead on a *Romeo and Juliet* love story that really needn't have been a *Romeo and Juliet* love story were it not for bungling British politicians.

Now from what I've written so far it does sound like a pure historical but of course it isn't. There were alien assassins there but, as in *Rosa* they turned out to be a token presence for a production team not brave enough to get rid of monsters entirely. They looked great and did whizzy things, but soon turned out to be the stupidest idea for a set of aliens in quite some time. Did I get this right: they go around accompanying people who die alone? How many people is that a day just on Earth, let alone the universe? There is no point in getting worked up about this stupidity; as I said, they are not for this story just for the viewers who might freak out by no monsters. And if you think I am joking then I can send you to at least one person who gave this 0/10 on Twitter because it had 'no monsters.'

So, this was a nice story, with an interesting little plot that fitted perfectly into the time slot. There were no duff performances, and it felt like we were in India. As I have noted it is getting clearer that the current production team have looked at all the evil in the world and concluded that humans are the bad guys and here, we have another story where a human is to blame. The brother is a little generically evil and it seemed to me that the writer couldn't bring himself to use the phrase 'radicalised' to justify his evil deeds (perhaps it is a BBC directive to not use the word). Whether we like it or not the idea that a 17-year-old lad would suddenly commit two murders in the name of a Hindu cause seems far-fetched and a Doctory explanation (like at the end of *Rosa)* to talk through some of the actual atrocities rather than a sentimental (albeit good) final scene might have worked. Whether (again) it was a clever idea for the baddie to just get away with being evil and for the crew to reset again for the next adventure also needs to be discussed. As with a lot of this series a lot of this seemed so bland, pointless, and tame.

Yes, the same problems persist here as has existed all season; I don't care what the production team say there are too many people in the Tardis, and they can't give them meaningful storylines: Graham and Ryan stuck doing little this time. Couldn't they have been left at home? Really disappointingly Yaz again does little except be the point of the adventure. Her police skills never mentioned, she has been wasted. I will say this, that after six adventures this is the blandest crew ever to be on the Tardis. We know nothing about them, and they are hard to care about.

This was very enjoyable, and I hope they keep going to the past, because the future has been a real lame duck so far.

Other famous reviews:

While it inherits several of the problems that have mired this year in controversy, it has an easier time papering over the cracks thanks to an intriguing alien mystery, a very relatable human cost and a setting which proves that, fifty-five years on, Doctor Who still has a lot to say about history and the people that made it - **Den of Geek**

It's a serious story told in a serious, almost stagey way. the parts that are strong aren't Doctor Who, and the parts that are Doctor Who aren't strong. And the non-Doctor Who parts aren't faultless either - Androzani.com

[This] shares a lot of DNA with *Father's Day*. Clearly the Doctor hasn't learnt her lesson – Daily Mirror

Ratings: 7.48 million (8th)

Ranking: 8/24

What have we discovered? History can be changed or can't um, I don't know anymore.

Title: Kerblam!

One Line Summary: Amazon is this week's target

Written by: Peter McTighe

British born but spent a lot of time in Australia and wrote the 6000th episode of Neighbours in 2008. He drifted towards Doctor Who and wrote a lot of the blurb found on the DVD releases in recent years. he got an email from Chris Chibnall, the showrunner on the iconic show's 11th season, who was aware of his work which included episodes of *Glitch, The Doctor Blake Mysteries, Winners & Losers,* and *Nowhere Boys.*

"My entire television career has quite literally been an elaborate plan to get to write *Doctor Who* – and no one is more shocked than me that it paid off."

He went on to write the acclaimed BBC series *The Pact.*

Directed by: Jennifer Perrott

Anything else before we start?

This was another early writers' room idea, although it was reworked a lot later. It had been pitched as 'our *Force Awakens*' but was toned down when the effects costs were realised.

The postmen idea came up quite late in the day. Early drafts were too full, with 'monsters, robots, massive spaceship sequences." Once they had been taken out (leaving only the setting and the bubble wrap) it didn't feel like Doctor Who so the Bots were added. Lee Mack's character was designed with him in mind, as was Julie Hesmondhalgh's.

The carpark scene was filmed in Bolton, according to McTighe, he said this when comparing the location shooting with his next episode, which got him to South Africa.

The Episode

There's no denying that this was the big win in this season and it's lovely to rewatch it. Doctor Who doing satire is rare - it's usual to mention *The Sun Makers* at this point - but this in its own way, is nearly as good.

The Tardis is avoiding a problem and the crew know what they're doing, which is nice. It's a space postman and Kerblam is the biggest delivery device in this galaxy. The gift's a fez and there's a note in it saying, 'help me.'

"Can't help to check can it, Doc?" says Bradley Walsh in the most phoned-in voice he's used for a while. They go to the space warehouse and get jobs going undercover using a double whammy of psychic paper and sonic screwdriver. Of course, this could be set in England and not be a Doctor Who story, but let's not quibble.

Lee Mack turns up and does Lee Mack's thing and we get eerie robots, and we all go 'Robots of Death!' and remember what happened to the robots then.

Some nice scene-setting stuff with the crew in various jobs. Clearly people are going missing, and the robots *are* eerie. Lee Mack takes a task off Yaz and looks worried. We hear his screams. We even get a jump scare. Wow, when did we last get one of those?

The Doctor starts investigating and via some fiddling finds that it was the system that sent the help message and this all turns on its head, slowly

A giant army of delivery bots, waiting to be delivered in one go. It's the packaging, the bubble wrap which will kill customer, and it turns out the maintenance man who is trying to sow seeds of robot incompetence is the bad guy.

Oh - and who killed the girl?

Verdict:

In the world of Doctor Who fandom the lazy reviewer's favourite trick is to lazily stereotype seasons or (these days) showrunners' eras into lazy sentences. There's a part of me that believes that Chris Chibnall knows this and wants to play us. This would impart on him a level of Moffatian mischief I suspect he doesn't possess, so it isn't likely, but the long-haul Doctor Who fan in me cannot help but keep looking for theme or trope with which to associate this era. All I keep seeing is a very safe television show made professionally and in a modern way, with no edge at all, as if it's being made by people who have been hired with no prior knowledge.

Yet Chibnall has a background in fandom and remember he was probably the most involved in active fandom of our three modern showrunners (Davies loved the show but was never going to rock up at Panopticon in a cosplay long scarf; Moffat loved it but with caveats – he knew it was uncool – and spent most of the nineties showing off about being the Doctor Who fan who actually worked in television – and… AND, Moffat doesn't *get* the show like obsessives do – I will still assert he still doesn't see it correctly, he misunderstands it). Chris Chibnall however was a member of a Liverpool fan club who met on regular basis to talk Doctor Who. They wrote fanzines. They were the core. They were me. Chibnall knows a lot of the times in the past when Doctor Who was out there being astonishing and blowing people away. From the *music concrete* early theme music, to regenerating actors, to scaring the daylights out of kids, he was there. There is none of that in his iteration. In fact, the thing that people are taking most from the first Chibnall season is that the episodes not involving him are far, far better than the ones he wrote. *Kerblam!* is no exception.

Writer Peter McTighe, on paper, wasn't an inspiring choice, almost the definition of a jobbing writer, picking up work on *Neighbours* in Australia etc. He made all the right noises in pre-interviews, saying all his career moves so far had been an elaborate plan to write for Doctor Who. And lo and behold he produces a winner when I wasn't expecting it.

After ten minutes I had my cynical hat on, and I was wondering whether this story was a rehashed script for a drama set in a huge mail order distribution hub and squeezed into Doctor Who. It didn't need to be set in space; the whole set up could have been set in Sheffield, or anywhere on Earth. The old school fans enjoyed the

Robots of Death-style eerie robots, and of course then moaned that they're 'doing *Robots of Death* with less beautiful robots. But the robots could have come from any point of the series: *The Greatest Show in the Galaxy, Midnight, The Beast Below* to name three.

Then you started to get into it: Lee Mack wasn't too irritating, but you pleased yourself by noting that it was going down an obvious route. And then you were stunned because you realised this was either very clever or accidentally very clever. Because if you've seen the *Robots of Death,* you know how this ends – and it didn't. That's not all, the second most plausible (nicked from the past) scenario – the corporate management evil (see *The Sun Makers*) was also hinted at hugely, and wow, that wasn't it either! We were completely fooled. So, when the actual protagonist was revealed the elegance of what we had watched was quite overwhelming. The misdirection was very clever indeed. And the bubble wrap, what a fine idea!

This allowed this episode to be a big win in my eyes. It kept the tone of the series, which is entirely the right of the current showrunner (and he isn't wrong – Doctor Who would have died with another Moffat season) but played a couple of very clever cards to catch us out. And modern parables like zero hours jobs are a great hook, but they could be bitterer. It's too nice.

There are still issues. Bradley Walsh looks bored, and his delivery of some lines was simply poor, barely more than reading them out. There is little empathy for the character. Not granddaddy enough for us to love (like Bernard Cribbins who took a similar role), but it is a way more experienced film actor, and not funny enough to defuse situations (could be the script). He has no purpose.

I know what they're trying to do with Ryan, but he still comes across as a character who is given things to do. He hasn't grown much in this season. Yaz was much better here, and I suspect a reduction in the Tardis crew to one might be the way forward, with Yaz retained. The three-companion crew doesn't work (my wife (a not-we) complained that there were too many characters).

Nobody has changed the gender of a character with a 55-year back story. If the character is now a woman, do you need a male character to balance? Does this young male fawn over the Doctor like four of the last five females did over male Doctors? Do you need someone who can do the rough stuff for the Doctor (a Harry Sullivan or Ian Chesterton) or is that sexist? IF you have a strong male does that change the balance? Could you have two females travelling through space and time? It's a difficult one to get right. Which is why I get the three characters they went for: a girl with skills because we must have one of those, a harmless but buff young man, and an avuncular type. They avoid all the traps, they do the job, but satisfy no-one. And the way they interact is not what this Doctor needs. They are all incapable of operating without the Doctor, so they are almost pointless.

And many have pointed out that the Doctor is picking corporate business over lone rebels here. Compare this to his/her more on the side of the rebels (see the one previously mentioned set on Pluto, and definitely *The Happiness Patrol*). After she let Jack Robertson off with a sort of humph then this is out of character.

"Systems aren't the problem," she argues, just people who "use and exploit the system" – thus refusing to engage with real-world suffering.

Cynical fans have been speculating about how the next season of Doctor Who will pan out. Some have suggested Chibnall's time is up and there is one maybe half a season left with him in charge (*Starburst* magazine and the Skaro web page to name two sources). It's alleged that Whittaker, Cole, and Walsh would go with him by Christmas 2019. It's hard to know, but episodes as fresh as this could be the way forward: with or without Chibnall.

Other famous reviews:

Kerblam! was very much a post-Eccleston Doctor Who story with Chris Chibnall's values ingrained, and proof that those two things aren't necessarily incompatible after all - Den of Geek – Chris Allcock.

A highly polished production with honed storytelling, all wrapped up in a neat package and delivered first class to your living room – Patrick Mulkern – Radio Times.

Time will tell if the show is starting to find its feet, but it felt like finally, here was a sense of who these people are. This is what the show should be aiming for every week – iNews.

Ratings: 7.46 million (9th)

Ranking: 4/24

What have we discovered? That misdirection is the hallmark of this era.

The Witchfinders

One Line Summary: Alan Cumming is camp, over the top and silly - but for a change, this is a historically correct interpretation

Written by: Joy Wilkinson

She started out as a business journalist because she had no idea how to get scripts made before getting in the BBC's Writers' Academy. Her previous plays included *Britain's Best Recruiting Sergeant, Now is the Time*, Fair and *The Sweet Science of Bruising*, about Victorian female boxers. She was selected as a Screen International Star of Tomorrow and wrote the BBC series *The Life and Adventures of Nick Nickleby*.

Talking about being chosen for Doctor Who, Wilkinson said: "I loved the show and felt like it might be a good fit for me, but I knew it was hard to get onto. So quite frankly I'm still pinching myself to be here!"

Directed by: Sallie Aprahamian

Anything else before we start?

Wilkinson was always a fan of Doctor Who (I know they all say that, but it is true in this case). She never expected to be able to work on the show, but a friend said her writing would suit Doctor Who. In the first writers' meeting she suggested "Pendle Hill rises up into an army of mud monsters."

According to Wilkinson, in early drafts of the script she started with the Tardis and had more build-up of there being something in the mud, little tendrils popping up to scope them out. (herocollector.com). Wilkinson said that Chibnall told her that Doctor Who was "sci fi structured like a thriller, written like a comedy, with the texture of horror." This suited her style and she felt at home.

Filming took place at Little Wareham Living History Museum in Hampshire, in 'absolutely brutal' conditions, according to Whittaker: the weather event was known in the UK as the Beast from The East, and it was cold.

The Episode

Another historical. Too many? They're in the past trying and failing to see Queen Elizabeth's I coronation, in England and there's a weird vibe in a forest. The Doctor does the 'don't interfere in History' thing again, yawn, make her do that on Planet Zog and I'll buy it. Masked people watch their progress. Bradley Walsh can recognise Pendle Hill from its profile, which is impressive for a Londoner living in Yorkshire looking at a Lancastrian landmark.

Surprise, surprise, there's a witch trial and a ducking stool. The Doctor stops it (Walsh's 'so much for not interfering is glorious and pertinent). It's clearly not Whittaker doing the speedy front crawl (we never see her dive in). The Doctor goes straight into the fight and argues with the woman responsible for the ducking (Becka) and the psychic paper says the Doctor is the Witchfinder General. Becka turns into a psychobitch murderer of 36 women and thinks horses are the Devil's work. I'll say this about the story - it's full on.

The Doctor and Becka have a bit of a religious argument and the Doctor cites the new King James translation of the Bible saying it is not what King James would want. And then Alan Cumming turns up as King James and this goes off on a weird tangent.

First, it's hard to get a grip on Cumming's performance. It's gloriously over the top, scene stealing of course, but probably in-character. How many viewers would know this and just assume it's scene stealing? It must be said that Cumming absolutely floors me when he called the Doctor a wee lassie. And his glorious flirting with Ryan, magic. And his assumption that Bradley Walsh is the Witchfinder General, also great.

"Careful, it's my pricker," is the puerile Doctor Who fan's favourite line since "Young men are dying for it," in *The Armageddon Factor* in 1978.

And then in the forest Yaz sees the granddaughter of the supposed witch and this goes all sci-fi. Some giant tentacles come out the ground. Yaz attacks them. Yaz find the Doctor and they go tentacle hunting.

Bradley Walsh and Ryan go with the King to get Witchfinder accoutrements. All you need to know is that Bradley gets a big bat, and they go witch hunting.

The Doctor finds some sentient mud and granny witch is back as a sort of zombie.

Everyone turns up as more zombie mud creatures turn up. The Doctor deals with them but is accused of being Satan's acolyte and is now seen a witch.

King James wants to know all the secrets of existence. And spars well with the Doctor. And the Doctor has a great speech about people. Makes no difference, off she is to be ducked.

Becka has a black mud tear; she is part of the mud people. But the Doctor does a Houdini trick and is not there when the stool returns to the surface. The mud creatures obey Rebecca. And this becomes about a tree she cut down.

They are an alien army, the Morax, captured and imprisoned for war crimes. And this is a bit of a shame as it becomes a bit scenery-chewing, juvenile bad guyness.

The tree was chopped down to make the ducking stool is an ancient alien thing to keep the aliens imprisoned. Billions of years old (er...no).

Fiery torches and a hilltop climax, a giant tentacle and the Doctor does everything with a very quick turn around

The final scene is great with King James wanting to take Ryan away and the Doctor quotes Arthur C Clarke. Bradley Walsh quotes Ezekiel but thinks it's from *Pulp Fiction*, which is also pretty good.

Verdict:

There's something slightly disappointing about *The Witchfinders*. It's because the high standard of the season's historicals has made the third historical of the season have higher expectations. Perhaps because it started very strongly and collapsed in on itself. Perhaps because Alan Cumming is simply superb as King James, genuinely one of the great guest star turns. Who knows, but *The Witchfinders* does find itself a little forgotten.

Chibnall blamed the weaknesses of *The Battle of Ranskoor Av Kolos* on having to do a lot of work on another script he didn't name. I don't have any inside information, but this might be it, given the strength of the other non-Chibnall stories. From the first scenes it's clear that great chunks have been cut to make it fit. The Tardis crew are already in situ with no preamble and we're straight into the action. And it's good action, a nice ducking stool scene etc. Alan Cumming shows up and it's all fine.

The problem is that this power struggle to repress women who were healers at the expense of qualified male doctors by calling them Witches is as horrible as the racism we saw in *Rosa,* but there the tone was serious and respectful and here we end up with a bunch of muddy zombies. The witches could have stood alone but of course that was never going to happen.

There is a modern trope for convention-defying stories. Skilfully done, it can be brilliant but usually it is not done well. Simon Pegg's film *World's End* and to a slightly lesser extent *Hot Fuzz* by the same team are examples of work that switches genres crudely in the middle. This bumbles along but is trying to do the same thing, then we get a few tentacles and some black tears. It would have taken the work of a moment to hint that this would happen, and they chose not to. And it doesn't work, even though the mud zombies are quite effective. And while we're at it, we could lose King James entirely and the plot wouldn't be affected. Imagine this without Alan Cumming.

Now, it must be said that writers new and keen will always do this to the Doctor Who format. It is textbook to write what you know but it rarely gets a chance to get to the screen. Usually, these sorts of stories are seen in the spin-off novels. And if you are going to do a story about witch trials then unfortunately it is going to remind the discerning viewer of the much better *Inside No.9* episode on the same topic (*The Trial of Elizabeth Gadge*). It falls far short in terms of both humour and horror. The excellent Steve Lyons story *The Witch Hunt*ers (set in Salem) from the BBC Past Doctors range is a similar idea, but not a source.

It's nice to see the Doctor's gender used as a plot point but it could have been more pointed. This is typical of the modern product, a reasonable enough idea confused in the realisation and without any oomph.

Other famous reviews:

Overall, *The Witchfinders* is a solid episode that took great care to go too dark for family viewing, or too comedic against that backdrop. Alan Cumming steals the show as most people knew he would. – Daily Mirror.

What we're left with, when all is said and done, is a pell-mell but flawed episode that abandons the history lessons in favour of an old-fashioned, monster-driven romp. If only the aliens had been given the same nuance, care, and screen time that the human villains have enjoyed so far, this could have been a classic episode. Instead, what we're left with is a passable story that not only highlights some of the shortcomings every script has suffered from this year, but struggles to define who, exactly, this Doctor is, not to mention her place in the universe she's defended all of her lives – Den of Geek.

An ineffective Doctor, loads of standing around and yapping. Horrific lurches in tone. Aliens only slightly more interesting than the mud they're made from. Watch it again? Thanks, we'll pick the ducking stool – androzani.com.

My biggest regret this episode? The lack of any "I would like a hat like that" jokes around the Witchfinder General hat. Way to pass up the wankiest continuity reference imaginable, Chibnall - Elizabeth Sandifer.

Ratings: 7.21 million (17th)

Ranking: 16/24

What have we discovered? That the best laid plans for historicals can so easily be lost.

It Takes You Away

One Line Summary: I can't unsee the talking frog.

Written by: Ed Hime

He won a Craft BAFTA for his first episode of *Skins* and won the Prix Italia for his radio play *The Incomplete Recorded Works of a Dead Body*. His work for theatre has included *Small Hours* at Hampstead Theatre Downstairs, *London Falls* and *London Tongue*. Politically active, he was arrested in London in 2019 being part of the Extinction Rebellion protests.

Directed by: Jamie Childs

Anything else before we start?

Ed Hime was recruited via executive producer Sam Hoyle. Hime was taken with Chibnall's explanation of what he wanted the series to be like and referred to *ET*-era Spielberg: wonder, innocence, scares, and real danger. As ideas were thrown around the Writers' Room Chibnall explained he might just pick a tiny piece of an idea and encourage the writer to focus on that. With this piece it was claustrophobic horror films and Scandi-noir. *Let the Right One In* (2008 Swedish vampire flick[4]) was a big reference for Hime, especially the setting. Also, *The*

---

[4] Dir Tomas Alfredson

Orphanage (2007)[5] set in an old orphanage where the son starts talking to an invisible friend.

In a later interview Whittaker was asked about her least favourite things was learning lines and on Doctor Who it was particularly hard. "When I first started, I'd get my pages, I went, 'OK, I'm not shooting for two weeks, but oh my god.'" "The first proper wobble was *It Takes you Away* and I had a massive monologue about the Solitract – three pages explaining something and I'm like…"

She has a system where she put lots of pictures up around the house and ran round learning it. She never lost the fear but learned to embrace it.

The Episode

The Norwegian fjord setting ticks the new places to go box. The Doctor is suitably kooky in working out where they are. Scanning a sheep and talking about the Woolly Rebellion better be a joke. They see a hut in the forest. It's too warm to be Norway in winter. A mild jump scare at the patched up and abandoned cottage sets the scene. Ryan and Bradley Walsh find someone in a wardrobe, Hanne is blind and scared and her dad is missing. She talks of monsters and there are traps and monster noises. "It takes you away," she repeats. This is all creepily effective, if weird.

Bradley Walsh and Ryan find a mirror that has no reflection. The Doctor as a look but she doesn't know

---

[5] Dir J.A Bayona (Spanish)

what's going on. The Doctor forces herself through to another world. They all decide to go through, but the Doctor interjects, and Ryan stays behind to look after Hanne.

In the portal it looks like *Pan's Labyrinth* but that's obvious. They encounter an alien called Ribbons and there is an anti-zone to keep threats away. Fleshmoths consume Ribbons and they go back, but this time it's a different house that looks the same. They find Erik, the dad and his t shirt is reversed (but you won't notice that first time around). And mum is alive. And if he leaves, she might go.

Of course, in the garden is Grace and Bradley's 'don't do this to me' is his best acting so far. Grace seems real. The Doctor concludes this is a copy world and it is dangerous. She then pulls Solitract out of nowhere to explain it all. It's like a kid with nuclear chicken pox and the universe cannot work with the Solitract in it so it was banished here. And they're in the Solitract plane, and it's lonely. The Doctor breaks Bradley's heart by saying Grace isn't real. Hanne isn't fooled by her fake mum. Grace shows her true colours. Whittaker is great as she persuades the Solitract to keep her instead. And then…

…we get the talking frog with Grace's voice. I mean the phrase 'on drugs' comes to mind. It all ends limply.

Verdict:

One of the hallmarks of Jodie Whittaker's first season was that a lot of the stories came from a Writers' Room brainstorm. Chibnall got his writers together and they threw ideas around: a very American idea, and a very good one. This story came from those discussions. It's a thoughtful episode that was trying to do something different, but the issue is that it is trying to do four quite different things in 50-minutes. They are:

1) Bring a bit of Scandinoir thriller action to Doctor Who – good idea.

2) Have a little recreation of *Pan's Labyrinth* – a good idea.

3) Have a way of connecting with 'the Dead' so that Bradley Walsh can have a dilemma – a good thing.

4) The baddies are suddenly remembered by the Doctor with no warning who manifest themselves as a talking frog – a very, very VERY bad idea.

When written like this you can see the problem, there's no connection between these ideas. The idea of an evil portal with an enemy that possesses you is Pyramids *of Mars* and yes that had a slightly duff part four too but not as duff as a talking frog. On setting alone, it gets brownie points, but we can't get past the frog, whose appearance has been called the biggest misstep since the Kandyman. As any old school Doctor Who fan will tell you, the embarrassing monsters in Doctor Who could be humiliating in the playground the day after and the talking frog must be the worst example ever. It brought back horrible memories. This is a victim of gut feel. They dropped the ball.

Having said that, this is another story that works very well on a later viewing. At the time you were blindsided by all the weirdness, jump scares and an assumption of monsters, the obvious *Pan's Labyrinth* vibe, the ludicrous Ribbons but once the heart of the story was made clear it's a really nice thing indeed. We can never really get over the talking frog (well I can't) and one day long in the future when modern Who is talked about in the same way as old Who is some crusty old script editor will explain the thinking, but then how do you display an entire consciousness/universe in a simple way? Nevertheless, in an infinite universe a creative team will never again produce a talking frog on a Windsor chair and for that we must give thanks.

Other famous reviews:

The first two thirds of *It Takes You Away* does exactly what it advertises, bundling you onto a roller-coaster of strange places and stranger things. Even if the destination turns out to be something of a disappointment, the journey itself is at least inventive enough to be decently entertaining - Den of Geek.

Metaphysics and *Doctor Who* don't always mesh – remember that interminable 2015 dispatch in which Peter Capaldi spend 50-minutes running upstairs shouting at himself? But *It Takes You Away* is thoughtful and big-hearted, blending scares and surrealism with aplomb. it stands unchallenged as the season's finest episode – Independent.

Sure, there are a lot of weak spots and faults. But dear God, what a relief it is to see an episode this season that manages to surprise, entertain, and hit some genuine emotional points. We're practically delirious with joy - androzani.com.

Ratings: 6.42 million 24th

Ranking: 12/24

What have we discovered? You think you've seen everything…

Title: The Battle of Ranskoor Av Kolos

One Line Summary: *Time and the Rani* written by the guy who went on TV to moan about the writers of *Time and the Rani*

Written by: Chris Chibnall

Directed by: Jamie Childs

Anything else before we start?

Chibnall said: "Particularly in that first series, I spent a lot of time helping other writers. We had some problems towards the end, and I had to go back and do some big rewrites, which meant that the version of episode 10 [*The Battle of Ranskoor Av Kolos]* that we filmed was a first draft. But I just didn't have time to do a second draft. It didn't feel enough like a season finale, and that was entirely down to time."

He continued: "So that's my least favourite script of mine. But I really attacked *Resolution*, so hopefully I made up for it with that one."

As many wags have noted, there is no battle in the story.

The Episode

The early scenes give me *Time and the Rani* vibes (by Pip and Jane Baker). Yes, the irony. But two aliens talking in plot exposition with eccentric hair in a quarry does that to a person.

Sci-Fi stuff happens and then we get the glorious caption "3407 years later." I bet someone worked for days on that precise number. But it might also so they can tell the limp 'Bet the last seven years dragged' gag later. The Tardis has picked up a distress signal from the planet Ranskoor Av Kolos. The crew land and Mark Addy points a space gun at them. He's playing an amnesiac called Paltraki, amnesiac only for plot convenience reasons it turns out. The Doctor gets some of his memories back. And Tim Shaw appears and, "wants what is mine."

It's a brave move to bring back a half-assed baddie from the first episode. Bradley Walsh gets his serious face on as he contemplates unfinished business of Grace's murder. The Doctor won't let him kill him. I mean the chances of Graham killing Tim Shaw is minimal, but the Doctor won't have him in the Tardis. I'm sure companions have killed people before. Leela definitely. And even a quick look and if we count Daleks and aliens like Voord as people we get (Ian 6, Susan 2, Barbara 6, Jamie 7, Ben 3, Zoe 1002 (it's complicated) I'll stop there). Where did this morality suddenly come from?

Ryan and Graham avoid death by two teams of robots opposite each other firing and ducking, thus killing the baddies. Why are soldiers of the future so stupid?

The Doctor meets an Ux, who is Penelope Wilton. This is descending into aliens talking about stuff and nobody caring.

Tim Shaw blames the Doctor for his fate and spouts some stuff and he is just like many other Chibnall baddies. Wait until the flux. Tim Shaw thinks he's a god.

The Ux do the eye thing from *42* and Tim Shaw goes on about the usual bad guy stuff.

Mark Addy's amnesia is a convenience to keep the plot secret. Tim Shaw targets Earth, well of course he does, to ramp up tension. Bradley Walsh blows up robots using a Bruce Willis line. The Doctor wakes the Ux up.

Tim Shaw meets Bradley Walsh. Graham's the better man although it contrived to make him shoot him in the foot and then there's comedy moments, as if they don't believe in it really. They lock Tim Shaw up for an eternity. The Tardis and the Ux do something, and the retreat is dispersed.

Verdict:

Chibnall claims this was a first draft and even so it's the weakest season ender since *The King's Demons/The Twin Dilemma* era Doctor Who when the concept was to front load the show and the last stories had no money spent on them.

You could at least ironically enjoy the *Time and the Rani* vibes and the cod science fiction. You could enjoy the telegraphing of the plot – amnesia and revenge against Tim Shaw, whom Bradley Walsh is better than. It's just such a pale imitation of the great stories of the past as to make you wonder why you are watching. The tone is all wrong, the Doctor serious, then not is fine as a thing, but it gets wearing because the viewer is confused by it. They haven't fully utilised the new dynamic and there is too little for four characters to do in 45-minutes. I mean here Yaz (again) just accompanies people and looks serious.

Tim Shaw from *The Woman who Fell to Earth* makes a vague threat to Earth from a far distant planet; we know this is feeble and we realise, at last what is wrong with Whittaker's first season, it's that the creative team seems to not understand suspense – at all. There is no tension, we know that all is going to be fine; we can even telegraph what is going to happen because the emotional journeys have been laid on with a jam spreader. It's predictable and although this is a blessed relief after years of overblown scenarios -sometimes it's human drama that makes a show – but it would be nice to have some kind of threat. And this isn't enough human drama. Yes Bradley Walsh, gets his moment to take revenge but it isn't played well enough for us to care.

Other famous reviews:

Beneath the fuss, though, this was a solid conclusion to a deliberate, methodical reinvention that stayed true to the values it's established this year as well as a few of the themes that have bubbled for far, far longer than that - Den of Geek.

We've seen a lot worse episodes than this one. And even the season isn't a total write-off. There are some redeeming features; there are plenty of *potential* redeeming features. But we don't want to have to overlook vast tracts of it in order to conclude that

it's good Doctor Who. Call us ungrateful, but we want mor
- Androzani.com.

It's soulless, pointless, and worst of all, it's fucking boring
- Elizabeth Sandifer.

Ratings: 6.65 million (18th)

Ranking: 21/24

What have we discovered? Season finales don't have to
be epic.

Resolution

One Line Summary: They remake *Dalek* and set it in Sheffield.

Written by: Chris Chibnall

Directed by: Wayne Yip

The only director to return from the pre-Chibnall era, Yip directed *The Lie of the Land* and *Empress of Mars* and had a hand in a few episodes of the Doctor Who spin-off, *Class*. He's since directed some of the weird Amazon Prime series *Hunters* with Al Pacino. He is now in the big-league and is executive producer and directing episodes of the Amazon Prime's *Lord of the Rings'* series, *The Rings of Power.* He was brought back by the producers because of his great visual flair.

Anything else before we start?

Chibnall fibbed through his teeth in pre-premiere interviews where he insisted that there were no old monsters returning for the new series. It was later ret-conned because this of course is a SPECIAL, but it was filmed with the rest of the series and was broadcast only a few weeks after the finale.

Chibnall went to town on this script because of the problems with the previous one. He was particularly proud of the scene between Ryan and his dad in the café.

He always felt 'specials' should feel like an opener and a finale all in one.

And for you location fans, Siberia and the tropical island bits were filmed at the same Welsh location: Newton beach.

The Episode

Well, we're back to doing pre-credit sequences are we? Voice overs too (but who is it) and somebody has been watching *Game of Thrones*. I mean what a ludicrous mess around with established history. Is this genuinely supposed to be our Earth? Having said that, it's novel and the segue from the corpse of the man who was bringing his bit of the body of the 'enemy' to the archaeological dig in a building was quite lovely. I'm going with 'good start' on balance.

There's a bit of shy, romantic talk between the two archaeologists, because they're geeks you see and can't just ask each other out. And then it all goes pear-shaped. An artefact seems to be being revived which makes the other bits revive.

In the Tardis they've been watching various New Year's Eve celebrations. All good. This is the best written episode for a while.

The artefact in the bag is alive and scuttles off. You know one of the archaeologists was going to get it from the moment of their awkward conversation. It looks like the female as she finds a squid like thing, which has gone when the Doctor arrived. They all go to Graham's house as a base and a convenient way to bring Ryan's dad into the story.

Yeah, you see, the 'squid' is attached to her. The CGI isn't super great. She is the squid's prisoner as the music goes all synthesised Led Zeppelin. The Doctor says the name 'Dalek.' Sorry, could have said earlier but, you know, spoilers.

Like a lot of things in Doctor Who the iconic things in it are not cast in stone and can be manipulated to be what the current show runners want them to be. It's been discussed before how Doctor who simply reflects society in terms of relationships to science, thematic thrust, even the Tardis is modified to be a fantastic machine by the standards of the contemporary viewer. And here we have a Chibnall Dalek, which is different from a Nation Dalek, a David Whitaker Dalek, a Saward Dalek, a Davies Dalek and a Moffat Dalek. This Dalek is erudite and evil, and you've guessed it, sounds like Tim Shaw and every bad person in the Chibnall universe. Pantomime villain style without the ha ha ha after it reveals the plans.

The chase scene with under Dalek possession is fun. We fans fantasise about being stopped by the police and saying, 'You are an enemy of the Daleks.' Chibnall was enjoying himself. But then he messes it up by having the cop's partner not paying attention and reading a newspaper. Who would do that? She'd be on her phone. And then saying, 'flipping heck.' I know it's a PG show but come on. The tentacles behind the archaeologist is a great scene although I think a police officer would go for the radio before screaming, at least I hope so.

Ryan and his dad are in a cafe that's actually open on New Year's Day. Small point but surely it would be either closed or massively busy, not empty including no staff. It's a nice scene but all I kept thinking was Sharon D Clarke who plays Grace was born in 1966 and Daniel Adegboyega was born in 1978, how is that working?

Dalek girl goes into an office as the music goes all grungy discordant. She finds a Dalek gun explained by a throwaway line about using the black market for alien tech. I admit I was wrong earlier about the pantomime villain badness - as it just laughed like a proper baddie.

And then we get the UNIT thing. It's suspended, pending financial review etc etc. This is a taken as a Brexit dig but it isn't. What it is, is Chibnall getting rid of things from the past he has no right to remove. In some ways the removal of old stuff is a good idea but then you keep the sonic and bring back Daleks?

The Dalek is making a case out of steel. Dalekanium reduced to history. The Dalek is remade. It's...ok, but the Doctor can now stop Dalek weaponry with the sonic. Sigh. How did the Dalek make its sophisticated tech with a forge? It has some banter then flies up through the roof.

Back at the Tardis we have common problem of this era: 7 characters all in the same space, with limited things to do. And everyone starts playing with wires in the Tardis like it's normal

The Dalek vs army scenes are cool, if limited by the same old argument: attack it from two directions. Where, in *Dalek* these scenes worked, here it isn't so epic, because it seems less believable.

We get a weird vignette with a random family moaning that the internet is down. The first example of this era being unable to truly project a threat to Earth in any way that seems real.

The Doctor knows the attack from two directions thing though and then the Doctor explains a weird thing that destroys the Dalek in two seconds, that's modern Doctor Who for you. The Dalek's got Ryan's dad for extra mawkishness. The Doctor sends it into a supernova, nearly taking Ryan's Dad with it.

And then it's fam stuff.

Verdict:

Sigh, the problem with Daleks is that when they appear in the show they become this monster threat and then become either silly or too familiar. See the madness of *The Chase* in 1965. See *Death to The Daleks*. See *Daleks in Manhattan*. Therefore, they need to be constantly rebooted, as if we've never seen them before. Now *Genesis* was a genius way of doing it. *Dalek* worked for a rebooted show, but *Resolution* is less successful. There is a need to redefine Daleks, certainly do them in a different way, and this Dalek that can scavenge its way back to a functioning machine is a perfectly good way of doing it. But why keep it secret that it's a Dalek? They are literally the second thing people think of with Doctor Who. The premise is all wrong. And by now seasoned viewers know that Daleks only work in three ways: lone Dalek, with Davros and they're grunts, or they're galactic superpowers in a space opera way. No other way.

This is also the time to talk about the politically correct ham-fistedness of this era. I could have put this anywhere but a story where a security guard, for a short time is revealed to be gay and is immediately killed off raised the hackles of the twitterati, also citing how older Black women (Grace) and Lenny Henry's mother get hardly any screen time at all before being bumped off. This is all true but it's utterly pointless too and avoidable.

Resolution worked well as a New Year's piece and was probably the best episode of Whittaker Who up to this point, it just wasn't great by the standards of previous stories.

Other famous reviews:

This is Doctor Who reduced to pure spectacle, with no job to do other than sell toys and they don't sell toys anymore. It still feels a bit off that a Dalek mutant can survive being chopped into thirds, taken to the very ends of the Earth like it's a video game superweapon, and then teleport its trifurcated tentacles back together because somebody slapped it on a tanning bed - Den of Geek.

Between intermittent radiant smiles and sharp one-liners, Whittaker's dominant note in the role is a sense of lonely responsibility – carrying the cares of the solar system on her shoulders – which the scripts keep underlining - Mark Lawson, the Guardian.

Amid a year of exciting television, the arrival of the first female Time Lord felt frustratingly low key. While I loved Jodie Whittaker's nurturing, off-kilter performance, the series as a whole fell short of expectation, swapping thrills and sci-fi sparkle for plodding history lessons and tedious moral lectures. [*Resolution*], which proved that the series' head honcho, Chris Chibnall, had finally got it right – Daily Telegraph.

Ratings: 7.13 million

Ranking: 10/24

What have we discovered? Daleks can be constantly reinvented.

Season 12

Spyfall

One Line Summary: Mojo back?

Written by: Chris Chibnall

Directed by: Jamie Magnus Stone (part 1)

He started his commercial directing career with Doctor Who. Back in 2013, he directed two mini episodes that appeared during the 50th anniversary. *The Last Day*, and *Clara and the Tardis*. He also did some Second Unit directing on *Nightmare in Silver*. Then was absent for five years.

Lee Haven Jones (part 2)

Exeter University graduate with experience of directing big tv detective dramas including *Vera, Shetland,* and *The Bay*.

Anything else before we start?

"Episode one, I would say, is our most lavish, location-filled, action-packed episode, I think we've ever done," said Chibnall.

On the new series he felt it was more of an exciting evolution. "It didn't feel like a different difficult second album at all actually. It felt like we had done what we wanted to in the first series and people had responded, more positively than we could have hoped."

On Whittaker on how she changed the way the scripts worked. "It becomes me watching the rushes and seeing what she's doing, and sort of nudging and going, 'oh she's really enjoyed that moment' or 'oh she's doing this, and I didn't realise she could do that like that' or 'she's playing this differently,' which is really exciting."

"So, it's the sort of unspoken tennis match across the shooting in a funny way. I'll lob a scene and she'll hit it back."

"There's a dialogue at the start and then there's not really a dialogue during the series, apart from everything she does, which I watch every day. And that's the joy of it: just thinking, 'oh she did that brilliantly.' Okay, I've given you something new. Oh, she's done that brilliantly too. And you really can't ask for anything more from a lead actor, and I say that hand on heart.

"She is extraordinary. I knew she was extraordinary having worked with her before. She's more extraordinary than I thought she was."

This was originally conceived as a one-parter before being expanded. Chibnall explained this was "what got me addicted to Doctor Who (as a kid) was the cliff-hangers." It filmed in South Africa again, which managed to be Australia and San Francisco. The M1 chase scene was on the A432 in Cardiff. The infinity scenes in Part 2 were re-shot because 'they weren't impressive enough'.

Part 1

We really have forgotten all the 'nothing from the past' ideas from last season, haven't we? Pre-credits are BACK!! And Chibnall clearly thought the bigger scope of the world shown and thrown away in *Resolution* was cool, so we get BIG CAPTIONS of well realised other parts of the world. Two spy like things and a sniper in Africa.

Back in Sheffield ordinary people with access to a time travelling device prefer to be at home. Ryan plays basketball and is found by stereotyped spooks. Yaz's dad gives us a Beatles' reference. Yaz gets the spooks too. Bradley Walsh is at the actual Doctor's. Our Doctor is fixing the Tardis. There were issues with this at the time, but I've forgotten what. Something to do with the Tardis can't have an underside with wires.

There's a car out of control sequence run by a sadistic sat nav. It's a strong start not necessarily Doctor Who strong but hugely watchable even if the sight of the Doctor screaming is never edifying

"C" of MI6 wants to see them. It's Stephen Fry. He assumes Bradley Walsh is the Doctor – it's good joke but of course we've done it already in *The Witchfinders*. He's the surrogate UNIT because they had to get rid of UNIT. As this is a spy spoof, we get the spy kit section. It's fine.

Lenny Henry appears in a picture as the rich baddie: Search Engine supremo Daniel Barton. Stephen Fry then gets it mid-sentence.

The Doctor and Graham go to Australia; Yaz and Ryan check out Daniel Barton. San Francisco doesn't look like San Francisco. Lenny Henry is enjoying himself. Australia does looks like Australia. "O" is obviously the Master but at the time it was brilliantly hidden. Yet the Doctor for the first time doesn't recognise the Master and doesn't know she's in a Tardis. That's wrong. There are things outside. White lights in human shape. They trap one.

Lenny Henry is only 93% human. Ryan and Yaz are secreted in the building. Lenny Henry summons the light creatures. Yaz is taken by one. She's not dead she's in a weird forest and she materialises in Australia.

Although this is good fun. It slows at 40-minutes, and you wonder if there is any real plan. "Alien spies," concludes the Doctor.

They go to Lenny Henry's California vineyard for a party. It's a genuinely great scene. Whittaker brilliantly Doctory. Henry and Whittaker have a nice spar, we have a bike chase, and the background music spoofs Bond. Don't drop the ball.

The Master is caught out and it's a sort of yes/no thing. Sacha Dhawan likes an ad lib direction. The matchstick throwing was a brilliant ad-lib apparently.

And then we get a cracking cliff hanger of a plane with no pilots and a bomb that goes off which should be brilliant but over egged by the Master telling the Doctor all she's knows is a lie and then we get a cliff-hanger of the Doctor taken out of the plane to the same forest where Yaz was.

Part 2

This is probably a suitable time to talk about the Chibnall era's approach to publicity. Throughout their time, they did a brilliant job of keeping secrets. In Season 11 this was less a problem as there were no reveal moments, yet the appearance of the self-build Dalek in the 'Coming Soon' was a genuine surprise. Compare this to Russell T Davies era where they did like to do a spoiler or two. This was really highlighted around the time that Davies was revealed as the new/old Showrunner and the Instagram and spoilers that were revealed was extraordinary after years of radio silence.

Chibnall's team did an even better job in Season 12 (as we shall see). Revealing some things like Cybermen and Judoon but holding back other things to cause genuine 'wow' moments. The reveal of the Master here is genuinely great, as is the Captain Jack moment in the episode coming up. He will go one step further in the final months of this era with the cunning use of reveals in the 'Coming Soon' bits. The sight of Sea Devil[6] was genuinely exciting even if the episode was less so. And the appearance of Tegan and Ace was even more so. It is one of the great successes of the era and deserves praise. Even if it hits ratings because people need to know to watch.

Back to this and, yes it was a great cliff-hanger and it's a good Master, so they are sure to drop the ball. *The Impossible Astronaut* springs to mind the last time they

---

[6] Spoiler

threw so much at an episode and that was too much for casual viewers. Ryan in the crashing plane finds a button with his name on. Oh no, timey wimey escape. Once they started doing this all tension was gone.

The Doctor is in a forest with a woman who turns out to be famous. Ada bloody Lovelace. She hears the word Kasarvin?

Lenny Henry and the Master are in it together. Again, Dhawan is excellent here, acting everyone off the screen.

We're back with Lovelace to the 19th century. Chibnall loves a bit of Victoriana. You can see from how *Spyfall* is set up how he messed up *Flux*. Lots of superfluous stuff (like Ada Lovelace) chucked at a basic plot and not enhancing.

Then to make it worse the Fam are back in England. That's a full 11-hour flight from San Francisco. Really?

Back in the past the Master turns up just to be irritating and all unhinged. The Doctor works out she's with Charles Babbage and Ada Lovelace.

The Fam are being chased their online presence being erased.

The Master is in World War 2, of course he is. He's a Nazi, of course he is. An Asian Nazi. This guy is persuasive. Psychic projection filters?

Because we need another angle. And we have Noor Inyat Khan, and the Doctor is under her floorboards. The Doctor does her Wikipedia summary for the viewers. Ada stares out into a burnt city with an Eiffel Tower and says, "I always wanted to return to Paris." I'm not sure she would recognise it given when the Eiffel tower was built.

Lenny Henry has his mother in a warehouse.

The Fam bits are played for laughs. Tone meetings people. The Doctor sends the annoying drum beat that annoys the Master. So, you create a new iteration but can only use the past. "You're not the only one who can do classic."

The Doctor and the Master meet on the Eiffel Tower. Quick Jodrell Bank reference, which is nice.

The fam finds Lenny Henry's dead mum.

The Master has carnage planned and tells the Doctor Gallifrey is burned in its bubble universe. The Doctor traps the Master.

The Doctor gets to the Master's Tardis (unlocked - handy). The plan involving famous British and American people involved with humans in history and eliminating them. That's classic Pip and Jane.

Lenny Henry sends a text to everyone in the world: humanity is over. We're past peak human. Then sends an app to re program humanity erasing their DNA

The Master comes back via living 77 years (I love a sort of *Curse of the Fatal Death* reference.

The Doctor tells us what she did to stop it rather than showing us. And it's all over.

The Doctor goes and changes time to do the save the plane thing. The Doctor removes herself from Noor's mind. Never seen that before.

The Doctor checks out Gallifrey. It's destroyed. The Master projects himself. It was him. I had to make them pay for what I discovered. They lied. The Timeless Child – what is that?

The Doctor looks genuinely shocked.

Verdict:

There was a weird amount of hate out there for Whittaker/Chibnall both before, during and after the first episode broadcast of the new season. As a fan in his 50s I was bemused; I accept the need for social media to be extreme but of all the tv shows, if there is one where you know there will be good eras and bad eras, it's Doctor Who. It changes, it is not one whole. No-one owns it. Look, I'm not claiming the show is more mine than yours because I've been around longer but if you are in for life then you must expect good times and bad times. There will be times when you stop watching for a while. But you come back, and you learn to grudgingly accept the stuff you didn't like. It's Doctor Who.

There is no real doubt about that *Spyfall* Part 1 was a pretty good piece of Doctor Who. It had everything you could want – intriguing set-up, guest stars, weird monsters, action, some funny lines, some Doctorish moments, a genuinely shock reveal and a sort of quadruple cliff-hanger that hasn't been seriously attempted for quite a while. What more could you ask for?

Yet there are obsessions and complaints about continuity? Continuity? Seriously – this is Doctor Who. Nothing happens with any coherence. You must relax. It doesn't have to fit together. If the Doctor wants to put the Tardis on a mechanic's winch and play with some wires, that's fine. If you want a better explanation for the Master appearing well, you're not going to get one. Enjoy the story, accept things move on. There were plenty of things to be annoyed about that have weight.

That said, this story worked up to the halfway stage. The companions – the major bugbear with this era - all had something to do (bar Graham, who just hangs around) and everything is ready to go.

The problem is that Doctor Who is littered with stories who can't recover from a fine cliff-hanger and *Spyfall* Part 2 dropped the ball. It was an interesting piece in terms of structure: being essentially both Moffatian and Daviesian at the same time. The use of multiple time zones and the going back in time to save her companions from a cockpitless plane was Moffat all over, but (and this is meant to be as damning as it reads) it is done with far less skill than the master of that style could manage in a heartbeat. The 'Gallifrey is destroyed' theme is much more Russell T Davies but again done less well. It's as if Chibnall has taken on board the criticisms of his first season and dare I say it, sold out to someone and made more 'traditional modern' Doctor Who. That someone could be the fans or but it's much more likely to be the suits upstairs.

Thankfully, despite the about turn in style, the second episode rolled along with great pace and was hugely enjoyable. Much more could have been made of the Henry Barton storyline which ended up being a standard 'aliens control or steal something modern and trendy' (see catalytic converters, fat cures and Wi-Fi) from previous seasons. Lenny Henry never convinced me he was a tech geek and killing his mother for no reason seemed to be a fine example character insight by sledgehammer. And what happened to him at the end anyway? Like a lot of Chibnall stories it just sort of faded away with no real conclusion.

The three companions had some good moments again but (and one time they will get this right surely … or deal with the problem) this time they worked as a three and although this did allow some actual dialogue and discussion, it didn't get us very far. There was also no real sense of jeopardy, even in cockpitless plane. Whether this is the writing or the acting or direction is still unclear, and it really shouldn't be unclear two seasons in. Look, there are still too many companions, and none quite have the heft for the job of being a companion. Yaz is still the best bet, Graham is a waste of space and Walsh still can't say a line convincingly for me. Ryan is ok but doesn't seem to be part of the action, just … there. He follows rather than leads. But I've fallen into the trap of thinking that's what companions need to be companions. Do they need character? I mean really, was Jamie (one of the iconic characters) much more than a likeable bloke in a kilt?

Jodie Whittaker remains a ball of energy, never serious enough but as Elizabeth Day argues in her 'How to Fail' podcasts, angry women are often ridiculed in public whereas male ire is seen as empowering. Chibnall and Whittaker are right to avoid it. But that leads to the core problem that if, as Moffat correctly pointed out, companions are 'exposition' and 'comic relief' well then, we don't have any humour from the companions (only the Doctor) and we don't need three of them for exposition.

And if Whittaker is avoiding fury, then we need a furious companion like Tegan did in the 1980s. We also have the issue (to my mind) that when you cast a woman as the Doctor there will be conversations about who the Doctor travels with: yes, all three current companions are brainstorm solutions to that problem but that doesn't mean we need all three.

The Master is of course utterly superfluous to the plot being there only to meddle in an alien invasion that was already being considered. He could have been omitted but that would have removed the only parts of this story that sparkle. It's good to have an evil person being evil for the sake of it and Sacha Dhawan takes the role and runs with it.

Which brings me to the on-going culture wars and how they relate to Doctor Who. Sacha Dhawan is of South Asian origin and as I noted in the section above, he plays a Nazi, and his ethnicity is hidden from other Nazis by a convenient 'perception filter.' And the Doctor as a sort of coup de gras removes the perception filter as she leaves, leaving the Master exposed to racism of the people he was impersonating. Some people have a problem with the morality of the Doctor for doing something so specifically targeted at skin colour. Now part of the problem is that in writing a story where the Master impersonated a Nazi you either know who is playing the Master and therefore you have messed up, or you write the scene then cast a BAME actor and lose your Nazi scene. Either way bad production decisions make the Doctor look bad.

Finally, the historical characters are not very real and history as a comedy theme park is back as well – after the promise shown with *Rosa*, this was unfortunate. Much as there was a squee moment to see Ada Lovelace she was no more convincing on screen than H G Wells was in *Timelash*. There is little evidence that Chibnall investigated the characters of Lovelace, Babbage, and Noor Inyat Khan to get them right, he just threw some obvious things at them and hoped for the best, although to be fair there wasn't enough time.

The bottom line was this was a fine adventure to watch – in the moment. It was easy to follow, inclusive rather than excluding and better than most of last season's vanilla stories. There is an interesting running theme and a cliff-hanger set up to run towards. Whether they can keep it up is another matter and whether after this lip service paid to the past Chibnall returns to type remains to be seen.

Other famous reviews:

If *Spyfall,* is any indication, this series of Doctor Who will make the show's year-long absence worth the wait – Den of Geek.

It is brash, bonkers, and unstinting – everything you want from Doctor Who, especially in the glum days of early January - The Independent.

What decisively sinks *Spyfall* is a really, really bad Doctor. Get that wrong and nothing else is right, and this is *so* wrong. We've had some Doctors we've liked more than others, but none of them have been as far from where the Doctor's character should be as this one. So disappointing - Androzani.com.

Ratings: 7.13 million (14th)

Ranking: 2/24

What have we discovered? New ways of telling stories on Doctor Who.

Orphan 55

One Line Summary: Aka Awful 4.9…or "Fur Coat and no knickers."

Written by: Ed Hime

Directed by: Lee Haven Jones

Anything else before we start?

We know Hime was arrested as part of the extinction rebellion protests so it is no surprise that he takes Global Warming seriously. In his own words: "However, once you accept the reality of the climate crisis, what "extreme" means gets altered. I remember the shock of reading the 2018 IPCC report and not understanding how the world outside could be carrying on as normal, striding towards disaster. It was a feeling of overwhelming despair, shame, and grief. Then XR appeared as if by magic, occupying five bridges in central London. I'd never seen a protest that was so audacious and clever! I started attending trainings and got involved with my local group, meeting so many brilliant, inspiring people.

One of the most important aspects of XR for me is that it operates on the basis of acting with love for this planet, and for our children and grandchildren, who face a life that will be so much worse than our own. That it is the context for everything we do, and it is terrifying – but it can also set us free to act."

The arrest itself was quite straight forward. Like anything new it was disorientating and being hand-cuffed and carried by six blokes oscillates wildly between fun and scary. But my overriding memory is of being surrounded by the friendly faces of rebels, and of being surprised at how relieved and proud I felt."

Before this, Hime was in the Writers' Room and an early version of this was mooted, although it had to wait for the second series. The idea that was worked on was called 'A holiday gone horribly wrong.' This was to have been Hime's first Who script but only got as far as a first draft. It was resurrected for Season 12. Hime was excited to be working with a bigger cast after the almost two set and small cast of *It Takes you Away*.

The exterior shots were filmed at that stalwart location for Doctor Who now, The Canary Islands, this time Tenerife. They filmed on Mount Teide and the Auditorio de Tenerife was used for the Spa. It's a concert hall of futuristic design. They filmed there in two batches: February for the wasteland and it was extremely hot yet when they returned in April to film the sunbathing bits at the spa and the weather was cold and rainy. Watch the show, you can tell.

Whittaker wasn't happy shooting in a tunnel as her biggest fear is a monster coming out of the dark and she kept losing it when she was supposed to be being brave,

The Episode

I should declare an interest before we start. I loathe *Orphan 55* and am dreading watching it again.

Bradley Walsh finds a free holiday coupon at a place called Tranquillity. The spa looks a little overcast and barren and Bradley Walsh doesn't take his cardigan off. An alien with a tail and a Birmingham accent greets them. This is the sort of thing Russell T did better. We meet a few more characters. Ryan gets an electric shock but it's a hopper virus, and you get the usual comedy virus symptoms. The Doctor sorts it and Ryan must suck his thumb. Ryan meets a pretty woman (Bella), also sucking her thumb after being infected. He's not an impressive chatter upper, but it still works; the power of being a fictional character. The Doctor talks her way into seeing inside the security. And she asks the important questions why would need to defend a holiday spa with an ionic membrane?

There's a huge, angry alien out there…

Bradley Walsh meets some aliens with green hair. This is ghastly. Aliens with no alienness. It's childish.

The fantastic Laura Fraser from *Breaking Bad* is doing it seriously, but it's like she's acting in a different show.

The Doctor fixes the membrane, and the horrible drooling creature is banished saving Ryan and Bella from their doom.

We learn that the spa is a fake location. There's a barrier around it. It's a fake-cation. There is no oxygen on the 'planet' outside.

The planet is 'Orphan 55.' And they're going to go out there. The outside location stuff looks great, but there are too many characters, as usual. Also, as usual the alien can breathe CO_2 but for what biological purpose?

Ryan's still ineffectively chatting up Bella. They've clearly given up on the Ryan/Yaz thing.

Time for the service tunnel option (you could have guessed that, although what it 'services' is not clear. And there are trees. Ooh, naked aliens standing upright with no genitalia. The people creating this have really lost the plot

Laura Fraser is just killing this and everyone else is having a wonderful time. It's a horror show.

Ryan and Bella teleport back. Bella has a backstory and wants to destroy the place. Of course, the teleport doesn't work now, so it's a long walk back. Oh, and Bella is Laura Fraser's kid and of course the Doctor inserts some pointless comedy to the scene.

They find a Russian sign saying Novosibirsk that the Doctor calls a 'Siberian' underground station. Well, it's a Siberian city and it does have a Metro but unsurprisingly none of the stops are the name of the city. And does that tunnel look like a station? It's a bit like calling Green Park on the Victoria line a South British underground station. Or that there would be a London Tube stop called London. Anyway, everyone freaks out because they realise it is Earth and I get all *Trial of a Time Lord* vibes, where a Marble Arch tube (with a teeny escalator) was a clue that Ravalox wasn't Ravalox.

Irritating fires are still burning in a CO_2 atmosphere. The Doctor's oxygen supply is done. She confronts an alien and gets it back and can now mind read. There the Doctor said it, they breathe CO_2 in and exhale oxygen, 'like a really angry tree' I mean this is just the worse science ever. WHY does it do that? It's confusing respiration with photosynthesis.

Oh, and I should mention that conventional weapons won't work in a CO_2 atmosphere either. A gun shot is a combustion reaction and needs oxygen. This is not science fiction, its idiots making a show called Doctor Who as a job, with no interest in making it credible and not even realising how dumb they are being.

And then this becomes a global warming is bad story. I'm sure this is written to some obvious adventure template, but the execution is abominable.

The way to escape is that the only fuel (which doesn't work) will be activated by the hopper virus. Well, that's a coincidence. I know Chekhov talked about if you see a knife earlier you must use it, but this isn't that's the fuel needed to be mentioned too. Especially as it's all technobabble. Then to fight of the Dregs (who hate oxygen but seemed to be fine in the dome's atmosphere earlier) they attack it with oxygen. Surely the BBC could hire one person who has heard of science.

Even the hopper virus' manifestation is a worm, not a virus. Bella sacrifices herself and Ryan is sad although she's clearly unhinged, but then her mum returns and all is well

And then just as one-story single-handed mangles any credibility the show has for science it then screws up its Doctor Who credibility too when the Doctor admits that this future for Earth was just one scenario. Are things fixed or not!! Are they allowed to interfere with Earth's history, or not? It's so stupid.

Verdict:

Often with a new Doctor Who story immediately as the credits roll opinion is polarised and you never get a true reflection of the long-term quality until much later. Not in this case, I'm happy to stick my neck out and say, without fear of contradiction that *Orphan 55* is an absolute stinker and is in the running for being possibly the stinkiest Doctor Who story ever made for television. The writer Ed Hime has shown he had a feel for scares with *It Takes you Away* but lost points for the talking frog. It's as if he was told 'Hey Ed the best bit was the talking frog, now go and write another Doctor Who.'

I look forward to every Doctor Who episode. Since the revival in 2005 every minute of new Doctor Who is a bonus. I don't want it to be cancelled. I don't want to dislike stories per se, I want it to be good, I have a lifetime invested in the show, but this story was so inept that I despaired. And I disliked it not because of the political message or any individual performances but just the whole concept, the whole idea of Doctor Who in this form is terrible. I have alluded to this before that I feel that the current creative team have no idea how to write 'space' stories and this was a fine embodiment of that lack of skill. Like *The Tsuranga Conundrum* last season this was full of terribly clichéd aliens designed by people who haven't given the alien design any real thought, with lazy assumptions that aliens will behave in a 21st century way rather than in an alien way. No thought (again) has been given to anything about their character beyond 'ooh we need aliens' because this show has them and absolutely no concept of consistency to the tone of the story. Why have green haired aliens if they are going to be just like humans? Why? You have comedy characters, serious characters, angry characters chucked at the screen that make no sense. No reason for existing except to fill up some time. Good grief, if in Doctor Who's second story in 1963 they could do great aliens and even the bloody Sensorites in 1964 were better than these something has gone horribly wrong. One of the aliens looks like Barf from *Spaceballs*. Comparisons have been made between this costume (which is very poor indeed) and the cat masks from the Russell T Davies era. It's a fair comparison and stark to be reminded of the unevolving going on.

The idea of being teleported to a holiday destination is a good one (although done to death - *Macra Terror, The Leisure Hive, Delta and the Bannermen, Midnight, Voyage of the Damned* to name quite a few) but once there though there is no time given to explore or get suspicious and immerse yourself -it's automatically and instantly dodgy and trouble is afoot. And despite the paradise location it never feels like one. The weather looks decided cold and breezy unlike say *Smile* (filmed in sunny Valencia) that genuinely looked gorgeous. Here they filmed in the Canary Islands that are notoriously windy.

Ryan's virus 'infection' is played for laughs and is only there to give us the worst written 'if you're going to use a gun in act 3 you must show it in act 1' idea since the notorious hexachromite gas of *Warriors of the Deep* - a story that this reminded me of - a lot (in the sense of a story that was ill-conceived, written to a series of Doctor Who clichés but missing the point of the show and a tacked on moral message that has come to define it). Also, the 'comedy virus symptoms goofing about' has been done to death on Doctor Who: Matt Smith and David Tennant have done it recently.

So, I wasn't engaged particularly in this crazily paced first ten minutes but once the alien invasion was stopped, I assumed that they were going to do something really clever and curveball away - like *Kerblam!* did very effectively last season. Now, in a way, it did but it wasn't a good curveball, more a *Truman Show* curveball. The drive into a toxic world looked great but no thought was given to the time frame or distances. They drove some distance at pace (that is the impression given by the direction) but then when they needed to, they could get back to the dome by a convenient service hatch in about two-minutes. And if there's a service tunnel why drive at all? We find out this toxic world (Orphan 55) is actually Earth (and the old fans all laugh because yes, we're back to Ravalox and the reveal is remarkably similar to *The Trial of a Time Lord*) running along a tunnel (last seen in *Flatline*). This is the same *Trial of a Timelord* that Chibnall so famously went on tv to slag off for the 'pointless running up and down corridors'). It's not good if the two Who influences so far are *Warriors of the Deep* and the first four parts of *Trial of a Time Lord*, believe me.

The Doctor runs out of oxygen (I liked the oxygen light things, but they were totally thrown away in this packed plot) and finds out (by plot device) that the aliens breathe in CO_2 and exhale oxygen. Aside from it being insanely stupid science (um why are they bothering to breathe in CO_2, the oxygen we breathe is to 'burn' sugar to make energy and the respiration process makes CO_2 and water vapour? It's unchangeable chemistry. CO_2 won't do that; it puts out fires. There is no purpose to the inhaling of CO_2 and it certainly isn't anything to do with photosynthesis (which was sort of alluded to). So, it just shows these people don't understand anything! And as this stupid science scene is going on in an only CO_2 atmosphere, with no oxygen THERE ARE FIRES BURNING IN THE BACKGROUND! What is supporting that combustion? There's only one chemical that'll do it (Oxygen). It won't be CO_2! And while we're at it how does having a nasal strip allow you to inhale oxygen? Or was it to save money on props and have no masks? (Answer – yes)

And after the heroes have escaped (which was never in doubt) then the Doctor moralises about destroying the planet via CO_2 emissions. Some have found that problematic. If that's the problem, you have with this then there is no hope for you. But don't worry about the Doctor moralising. The show has been political forever, but it can be done with style: *Oxygen* a few years ago is a fine modern example. This was just 'CO_2 is bad, so there.'

Orphan 55 was inept and careless. It's disrespectful to science fiction storytelling, its execution and storytelling level was poor and childish by any standards. It's as if the makers think that all of that geeky stuff is beneath them, and it isn't and none of it matters.

This was disrespectful because it didn't cross the minds of everyone making it that it was a pile of childish, nonsensical clichés and lazy storytelling with the underlying feeling that (deep down) the producers and creatives have absolutely no idea what they are doing. This was done on the cheap but pretending it's expensive (how often are the aliens in shot with humans?) when a good story could be done on the cheap. It had hints of *The Doctor's Daughter,* another spacey clunker but at least the idea behind that was quite clever.

This took over from the previously mentioned *The Tsuranga Conundrum* as the lowest rated Doctor Who story on IMDB of all time and it's not wrong: 4.9 out of ten. This could be the worst Doctor Who story ever made. Time will tell. What a shame because nobody wanted to make the worst story ever when they got up in the morning.

Other famous reviews:

It's hard to find any redeeming features in this. Basically, it's sludge all the way down - androzani.com.

Orphan 55 is not exactly subtle about its climate crisis message, but writer Ed Hime has a blast getting there, with a zingy script about an apocalyptic future Earth brought low by "global warming, the food chain collapses, mass migration and war" and populated by horrific, fanged mutants known as the Dregs – The Guardian.

Reviewing it ends up feeling a lot like when I did comic reviews—that immensely frustrating sense week after week of going "you are failing at the most basic tasks of actually telling a coherent story." Except comics are a low-paying medium run by companies more exploitative of both employees and customers than usual in which the reason people work is usually fannish love instead of actual talent. This is BBC One in the age of Peak Fucking Television, and it leaves you wishing they'd go hire Dan Weiss and David Benioff, who at least understand what earning your dramatic payoff should look like in the abstract, even if they can't actually make it work. This isn't even broadly shaped like coherent televisual narrative—it's just vomiting a random set of concepts at the screen and hoping a point comes out somewhere - Elizabeth Sandifer.

Ratings: 5.38 million (5th)

Ranking: 23/24

What have we discovered? It can't get any worse (however, see the ranking).

Nicola Tesla's Night of Terror

One Line Summary: Eclectic Boogaloo.

Written by: Nina Metivier

She is a Stockport Grammar School alumnus who was inspired to write by *His Dark Materials.* She started in tv as a script editor at Kindle Entertainment. With Dan Berlinka she wrote many episodes (71) of *Dixi,* but also produced it, which won a BAFTA. She was Script Editor on some of the scripts from the previous season (*The Woman Who fell to Earth,* and *It Takes you Away*). Her favourite Doctor Who story is *The Girl Who Waited.*

Directed by: Nida Mansoor

Graduating in Politics from UCL in 2011 Mansoor started as a runner in Soho before joining CBBC and moving on to direct some episodes of *Dixi.* She was also credited with *We Are Lady Parts* as a writer. She was looking to get into 'genre stuff' so Doctor Who was a dream job to land.

Anything else before we start?

Metivier felt Tesla was a fascinating figure with manners were old-fashioned. She admitted she had a lot of mad ideas, and the CGI and costume people made them work. It was filmed in Bulgaria's Nu Boyana studio on the set of the New York streets. Doctor Who had also used this facility for Capaldi's *The Return of Doctor Mysterio.*

Robert Glennsiter, playing Thomas Edison watched some film of an older Edison so he could get a feel for the mannerisms and voice. Goran Visnjic, being Croatian knew Tesla as a hero in his native land and wanted to do him justice.

The Episode

The opening shot of Tesla trying to get funding for his power station by Niagara Falls is lovely. They didn't film in Niagara Falls so is it back projection CGI? (it is and it reminds us of what they can do – it was filmed at a waterworks building on the Cantref Reservoir). Tesla fails to get funding and is also letting slip something about Mars. Someone has died by one of his machines. As Tesla investigates, a green orb floats around. The Doctor bursts in.

The Doctor brings Tesla and secretary on a train to New York. Only the Doctor has heard of Tesla who she calls a genius. They jump trains to avoid the green laser shooting thing that is now shooting pink light. It's a human with a moustache and red eyes

In 19th century New York seamlessly showing the Brooklyn bridge and the Stature of Liberty then panning down to the Bulgarian film set for the street scenes is brilliantly done.

Question: the fam all does the 'dress up because we're in the past thing,' so why doesn't the Doctor? And why don't they dress up in space clothes in the future? Genuine questions. The answer is that nobody is thinking it through from a logical perspective. The Doctor Who tropes are so ingrained now that it's just the way it is. There is no attempt here to pretend they are from the time. None of the tension from *Rosa*. It's a theme park.

There's a nice scene where the Doctor explains the green orbs and we get some nice Tesla background too. It's done well. Thomas Edison shows up. The story about the 50,000 dollars is apocryphal but fits with the story as presented. It's more likely Tesla met Edison only a few times.

They find the corpse of the real person with the red eyes. They work out it's aliens and the aliens want Tesla (errr really?). This is Pip and Jane Baker levels of Earth science-centric egotism, and then we see a spider like we last saw with *The Runaway Bride* (it's a coincidence – by the way). The Doctor takes Edison into the Tardis, and they work out the green orb is a bugging device. Edison and Yaz are on a spaceship and the Doctor teleports up there. And immediately notices the Queen is a scavenger and steals tech rather than making it. All fine and dandy, if a little one-sided for an alien.

The Doctor has a plan to use Tesla's Wardenclyffe tower, beautifully realised here even though it wasn't finished in 1903, and in fact was never finished. Ryan thinks he invented Wi-Fi.

Yaz gets to behave like a police officer. This is often seen as a vindication of her, but anyone can make people move inside. The implication is that this is happening in Manhattan, but the tower is 81 miles away in Shoreham, on Long Island. There are giant scorpions on Earth. The Doctor has a shield. Minor peril is put in place. A double cross and it's all done.

Verdict:

There are two important things to talk about. One is the historicals, but the other is the new writers that have come in with Chris Chibnall. The main thing to highlight is: there are so many of them. Now I'm no conspiracy theorist (ha) but if you asked any of the old Script Editors (Douglas Adams, Terrance Dicks, Chris Bidmead) they would almost all agree that finding people who could write Doctor Who was almost impossible. It's too specialised. Let's look at some facts from 1970 onwards:

Season 7 – One new writer

Season 8 – two new writers (one in tandem with the producer)

Season 9 – no new writers

Season 10 – no new writers

Season 11 – no new writers

Season 12 – no new writers

Season 13 – one new writer

Season 14 – one new writer

Season 15 – half a new writer Antony Read (David Agnew).

Season 16 – two new writers – but one was, um Douglas Adams.

Season 17 – no new writers

Season 18 – five new writers (woo hoo)

Season 19 – four new writers (but two had directed before)

Season 20 – one new writer

Season 21 – one new writer

Season 22 – three new writers

Season 23 – no new writers

Season 24 – three new writers

Season 25 – three new writers

Season 26 – two new writers

Many seasons had one or no new writers which implies that many times established writers did the heavy work and/or new writers were hard to find. With Chibnall nobody had written a Doctor Who story before (OK,

Malorie Blackman wrote some fiction but not for tv). Sheer weight of history suggests that finding people who can write Doctor Who is harder than it looks, so either a) Chibnall is incredibly lucky, b) Chibnall is very skilled at finding these elusive writers c) Chibnall assumes any 'good' professional writer can write for Doctor Who.

It's clearly the latter and this is misguided. And this is a prime example. I don't think there are enough original ideas here with this script. It feels generic Doctor Who, like the whole of this season has felt like generic Doctor Who. I will say it again but ejecting all the people who have proven they can write Doctor Who is a major mistake. The new writers all say they always loved Doctor Who their whole lives, but did they really? And do we want writers who've always loved Doctor Who? Robert Holmes didn't. This script is the sort of by-numbers effort a professional writer would produce. Famous historical figure, some aliens after some kind of McGuffin. Think about Magnus Greel and his motivation nearly fifty years ago. Think about Jingo Linx.

The other thing to talk about is modern historicals, obviously because this is a modern historical but also because they were the standout success of last season. Back in the day, Russell T Davies used historicals as a way to tell stories with a different tone to the spacey ones and given that he was acutely aware that science fiction meant 'cult' and possible low viewing figures he was happy to go historical in the early days. His stories usually involved an encounter with a famous person and these famous people were almost always the famous figures Davies found interesting: i.e., writers. The historical setting was usually irrelevant, and the stories could have been set anywhere. What I mean by that is that the Gelth story in *The Unquiet Dead* could have been set in space or in the present day (with some tweaking). The historical was merely a cute background that would work because the BBC can do period drama well. This rule applied less of course when they were written by Gareth Roberts; with his stories every possible witty related concept to the famous writer was used to push the plot on, so in *The Shakespeare Code* the shape of the Globe theatre is a big plot point, and the villains are three witches. You get the idea.

Steven Moffat's approach to historicals was to also have famous people but to make them as cool as possible (which was often his approach to every character), so Winston Churchill is benignly affable, not too racist and *au fait* with time travel. Queen Nefertiti is a feminist minx, Madame Pompadour is otherworldly and hot, Queen Elizabeth is both otherworldly and a feminist minx and Robin Hood is too good to be true. The past is usually a euchronic comedy background often dwelling on Victorian cliché. There was no depth, no serious attempt to do a Doctor Who historical, more use the past to twist stories into shape.

Both showrunners also had the habit of shopping list historicals where a hapless writer was given a series of tropes and cliches to include in the historical. There was *Daleks In Manhattan* with Davies' strict rules as to what could and couldn't be in it, or *The Curse of the Black Spot* which reeks of pirate obviousness, and *A Town called*

Mercy which is shot-for-shot a Western movie rather than set in the west.

Chibnall, as we know reimagined the historicals and *Rosa* and *Demons of the Punjab* were fine and serious efforts to tell Doctor Who stories set in the past. Rosa Parks is never cool and sassy for the sake of being cool and sassy, the past is not a euchronic background, the past is nasty and crude in a way that alien worlds never seem to be. Yes, *The Witchfinders* was a little more traditional and all the worst for it, but it wasn't that far out there. The only real criticism of the three (yes three – that's more historicals than the show saw for 10 years between 1967 and 1976! I am NOT counting *The Time Monster*) stories was just the lack of bravery to make it purely historical and we had some token and forgettable alien threats. All well and good, therefore it is disappointing to see that this season they did not build on this success but instead someone has decided to chicken out of the brave (not necessarily good) decisions made with the last season.

We've noted how *Spyfall* was much more like a Moffat story (and his use of a cool and sassy Ada Lovelace and Noor Inyat Khan there was Moffatian too) and this Tesla tale could easily have been made under Russell T Davies. We have a big-name actor playing a famous figure from the past and the Doctor being in awe of him, reeling off achievements etc. The aliens are front of house and looking for Tesla – he is essential to the plot (ish); there is much less of an attempt to portray early 20th century USA properly. Yes, it looked good, but this was the euchronia of the Moffat era. The skin colour issues in

Rosa are completely ignored, for example. Would Ryan and Yaz really have been treated so courteously?

But the euchronia isn't the issue with this one; that the series is happy to attempt a turn of the century, set in America story is impressive enough. No, the problem here is the lack of ... I don't know ... inspiration. You have Nicola Tesla who people have heard of because of the cars (although no reference was made to this obvious thing at the start– and eventually fixed by a quick line from Ryan), the other thing people will know are his beefs with Thomas Edison and if you know anything about these two, well they are what you see on screen, we get the dogged inventor and the stealer of ideas. The real crime here is that this goes down the Gareth Roberts' route where the things we know about the historical character are seen in the aliens. As Edison stole Tesla's ideas these aliens steal technology. They're not inventors like pure, perfect Tesla. They need Tesla to make their ship work. Much has been made the alien Skithra's startling resemblance to the Racnoss in *The Runaway Bride*. It's awkward but could it perhaps be an ironic stealing of another costume (like the characters steal tech)? This would be in-line with the one characteristic these alien scorpions have - magpies. If so it's a bit 'meta.' Unfortunately, the only explanation for this identical costume is the meta one. Anything else implies rampant ignorance on behalf of the team or blatant copying. I'm sure neither can be true so it must be done with knowledge. Having said that, the ignorance of the current team to historical Doctor Who might mean that this is a huge coincidence.

Despite the fine appearance of this story this is the weakest of the Chibnall era historicals, but even as the weakest it still picks the show off the floor after the previous week's debacle and was at least OK to watch. Given that I was still reeling from the previous week's story and felt I could never watch Doctor Who again I was a little scared and that brought my enjoyment down. It might even be good if watched out of sequence.

There is still the feeling that they are throwing anything at the screen at the moment but desperately trying to find a winning formula but don't really know what is good and bad Doctor Who. The policy of discarding everyone who knew how to make Doctor Who is flawed and those who are new only seem to know Doctor Who in a Chinese whispers, despite them all professing to be huge fans of Doctor Who, sort of way. There's no attempt to redefine Doctor Who they're just making 45-minutes of television like the good television professionals that they are. The heart is gone but the corpse is still moving. The show cannot go on like this. There's no point to it.

Other famous reviews:

At some point along the way, someone seems to have found a copy of *The Runaway Bride*, spotted the Queen of the Racnoss, and declared "everyone ruddy loved that character, let's do her again!" - Den of Geek.

We can see that it also has some things going for it, especially in the character department, and in the main it's a nice flowy watch. We've seen a lot worse, and not that long ago either. We'll take it - androzani.com.

It was hardly a reinvention of the wheel – or indeed the lightbulb – but *Nikola Tesla's Night of Terror* succeeded in what Doctor Who's historical episodes do best: painting an entertaining, educational and poignant portrait of a figure that the history books left behind – iNews.

Ratings: 5.20 million (6th)

Ranking: 15/24

What have we discovered? The production team have short memories.

Fugitive of the Judoon

One Line Summary: Sleight of hand.

New Cast:

Jo Martin – The Doctor

Born in London she was quite the jobbing actor, appearing in *Doctors* and *Jonathan Creek* and *Casualty*. She got a more substantial role in *Holby City*.

John Barrowman: Captain Jack Harkness

Born in Glasgow he moved to the USA when he was eight where he acquired his American accent (it turns into Scottish when talking to his parents). He first appeared on television as a presenter on a children's Saturday morning tv show called *Live and Kicking,* but he established himself as a musical theatre performer. Cast as Captain Jack in the first season of the revived Doctor Who he had the spin-off *Torchwood* to lead, and he became somewhat of a national treasure.

Written by: Chris Chibnall and Vinay Patel

Directed by: Nida Mansoor

Anything else before we start?

The idea for this came from the Writers' Room for season 11 and the idea of a fugitive in hiding was one of the earliest ideas discussed. McTighe remembers an early idea about a vineyard in Spain, which Wilkinson thinks 'was an early prototype of *Fugitive of the Judoon,*' and the vineyard idea was transferred to another tale. At first it was just a chase after a stolen princess, but Chibnall had other ideas and Patel went with it.

It must be said that there was a lot of misdirection in the previewing of this. Patel was quoted in *DWM* as saying this is 'lighter in tone' but it was all misdirection. Chibnall suggested the Judoon. Patel researched them diligently – i.e., he watched *Smith and Jones*. He also liked the idea of a cathedral city sci fi story because he had studied at a similar city to Gloucester (Exeter). There was a lot of love for the Judoon on location from fans.

Martin had 'no idea' that she was going to play the Doctor and just auditioned to play Ruth. If she had known she would have 'flopped' the audition.

Captain Jack's appearance was added later once Barrowman was confirmed for the New Year Special. The idea took hold to 'smuggle' him into this story as a cheeky bonus. He was credited as Roy Lester (both character and performer) on the call sheets to keep the secret.

The Judoon captain is called Pol-Kon-Don in memory of friend of Chibnall's who died in 2019 (Paul Condon).

The Episode

Of course, it's all a confidence trick; from the title to the way it's set up. It's designed to make you look the other way. You shouldn't dissect tricks because you ruin them, but this is so clever I forgive them.

The opening scenes of a regular woman (Ruth) getting ready for work is vintage Russell T Davies normality. The cynical viewer sits there moaning, 'it's a Davies' era rip off.' Then, it slightly switches focus to the husband, and you switch to 'suspicious.' You're being led by the nose. Ruth is a tour guide at Gloucester. She's not successful. She's also turning down a guy at the cafe and further suspicion is heaped on the husband.

The Doctor is being self-contained and it's good to see her affected by things. Yaz asks where she goes when she says she'll be 'back in on hour and never is'? Um, scriptwriters, she's a time traveller, she can choose when to return.

The Judoon arrive and are the second sleight of hand. Everyone loves them but seeing them further enhances the retro, 'it's shit, and they have no new idea vibes' (perhaps also seeded by the Racnoss-not in the previous story). The Judoon put an enforcement beam around Gloucester. They are cool. They are cataloguing everyone. The 'fugitive' is there. All suspicion is still on the husband. Ruth finds an alien box. Bradley is zapped. The coffee shop guy is zapped. But Bradley reappears somewhere and bumps into Captain Jack. At this point people punched the air. Of course, but it's the first sign that this is weird (it's a beautifully kept secret). Captain

Jack thinks Bradley Walsh is the Doctor (third time they've done this joke now) and tells him the future of the universe is at stake. And 'beware of the lone Cyberman.'

The Doctor thinks the husband is the fugitive too, but, both him and Ruth pass the scan as completely human. The Alliance have come back, but the box is causing the husband to be bothered. The Doctor is told to take Ruth with her and goes all suspicious. Commander Gat materialises and knows the husband. She kills him. Ruth gets a text and a weird vision of a lighthouse. The biological shields are down, and Ruth is identified as the Fugitive. It's the usual crap sci fi explanations but the early trick was done so well you don't mind. She's a butt kicker.

"Follow the light break the glass." Ruth knows it's the lighthouse she grew up in. The Doctor accompanies her to the lighthouse. It's abandoned in that television way of not really feeling abandoned. The Doctor goes searching and goes to the light room and sees a grave and Ruth finds the break glass thing for setting off alarms, as the Doctor digs up the Tardis by the grave. I mean, that is one of the great reveals in the series. Much as the Chibnall era is divisive, much as how it went from here. digging up a Tardis and revealing an unknown incarnation of the Doctor kicks ass. This is gripping. Don't see why the fugitive Doctor needs to immediately dress differently though. It's a proper old school Tardis console too. Much cooler.

The Doctors are confused and bitch about each other's dress sense. The Jo Martin Doctor was hiding from Gat. The Doctors meet Gat again. The Fugitive Doctor tricks her. She's a Gallifreyan too. Then it sort of ends with the Doctor being a bit dark and 'you don't know me' to Ryan.

Verdict:

First, the nagging feeling I'd been having about the behind-the-scenes stuff was confirmed. I'll explain; during the off season I suspect that the Producers were hauled into some bigwig at the BBC's offices, were told to buck their ideas up and were reminded how successful the show was under Russell T Davies and why don't you try and replicate that? Therefore, it seems the team have carried out the order to the letter.

Anyway...I was settling down for another disappointing episode, another 'watch because I'm a Doctor Who fan' fifty minutes. I wasn't expecting to actually enjoy it. I was fooled and not in a bad way, in a 'thank you producers' sort of way. How could a Doctor Who fan **not** enjoy *Prisoner of the Judoon*? You've seen it, you know what I mean.

This feels like a Chibnall episode but it's co-credited to Vinay Patel. It feels like Chibnall when he wrote for Doctor Who rather than ran it, in that it's heavy on the lore, if a little stilted in the execution. It started off as a workmanlike, a sub-Davies normal human life sort of episode, which I could live with, yes it felt a bit weird in context with other stories of the era, but I was fine with what we saw.

Oh heck, who really cares? The great success of the Chibnall era is his ability to keep secrets, the production team's desire to completely floor fans consistently. We knew this, and this episode absolutely confirmed this. It was extraordinary. The Judoon deliberately used in the pre publicity to fool us into thinking one thing and hiding the shocks that this episode was really about. At the time I thought - there, old Daviesian one-dimensional monsters coming back and being better than any of the new monsters - but we were supposed to think that. Even the 'who is the alien?' was a delightful sleight of hand as the early scenes suggested a sort of *Hitchhikers'* Ford Prefect vibe but that was a feint as well. Then Graham gets teleported and that voice in the background sounds like Captain Jack. Dammit, this team has no clue about the history. Oh, it IS Captain Jack. And I was sooooo pleased to see him. Then once we got past the compulsory Jackness and you start to relish expected hilarious flirting with the now lady Doctor and then he doesn't even meet her at all and just passes on a message. Will he return? He must.

And then Ruth, an alternate (past?) version of the Doctor, and a cold, calculating one too. The reveal again was extraordinary. We knew there was something going on, but the Tardis buried under a gravestone reveal was another cracker. You can make a case that Doctor Who is just a series of iconic images and memories – well this story seemed to take this idea and totally run with it. The buried Tardis was brilliant. You start to question what you know about what is going on. It's brave, cult, niche television and the fans will love it. What about the general viewer though? Is this going to alienate? The answer is 'of course' and it was what Davies was always scared of.

There will be a price to pay, and this is the price of someone telling the production team to do a Davies.

Whittaker gets some acting to do at last. She shelves the kookiness, and broods, gets secretive and my goodness it is a welcome sight. The slight prickliness between her and the fam, the reluctance to engage is just ... better for the character, it feels right for the first time since Whittaker's been in the role. I've discussed before the need for a female Doctor to find something different to emote because they can't do anger and rage without triggering stereotypes, and the whacky eccentric isn't really convincing so this closed and hurt version of the Doctor is quite brilliant and it would have been great to have seen it more often before.

Now, there is the reality that whatever is going on is going to be resolved in a boring and irritating way. The Ruth Doctor cannot exist without serious retconning, and so will be forgotten about at some point in the future. And it must be said this reminded me of *The Next Doctor;* watching someone else prance around being the Doctor in ludicrous clothes is always wrong and it feels wrong, and I can't work out whether that's deliberate acting choices or us, the viewers simply rejecting the imposter. And Whittaker stepping up and leading, as well as a reminder of the quality of previous companions with Captain Jack, further confirmed what we all know deep down – we have too many companions, and they aren't exactly vintage. As a pal in the pub said the next day (and after an exhaustive and wonderful conversation on all the old companions (fancying them was a decreed a valid character trait)) we concluded that the Fam as a collective is not a vintage

Tardis crew. Even Mel was above them because Langford was trying and therefore Dodo was the only serious competition at the bottom.

We have been here before, a huge revelation conveniently forgotten. I remember the Valeyard in episode 13 of *The Trial of a Timelord*, which was a similar wow moment, with not many viewers. I suspect it will be used to create a monster finale that will underwhelm, but praise where praise is due, that was fun and a very slick story. It just isn't a story that can be shown on mainstream BBC1 on Sunday night for much longer. This could be the day we remember Doctor Who was all over on tv again.

Other famous reviews:

For now, we have a story where the Doctor spends most of it outsmarting villainous cops, where a middle-aged black woman gets to be the Doctor, where we get to see Whittaker's Doctor on the back foot in a justified way instead of because she's mysteriously unwilling to actually stand up for anything, and where all the plot beats feel basically earned. I'll take it – Elizabeth Sandifer (Tardis Eruditorium).

We'll try to hold off absolute judgement until we've seen everything play out, then, but for now, we're happy to say we're more excited about what's to come in Doctor Who than we have been for a while – Starburst.

And yet, as a piece of event television, as a roller-coaster of the unexpected, *Fugitive Of The Judoon* absolutely works – Den of Geek.

Ratings: 5.57 million (6th)

Ranking: 1/24

What have we discovered? This show can still be magic.

Praxeus

One Line Summary: Contact has been made (you know what I'm saying).

Written by: Peter McTighe and Chris Chibnall

Directed by: Jamie Magnus Stone

Anything else before we start?

Starting this story in the middle with everyone split up structure was deliberate and caused problems. According to McTighe 'it had a different energy because of the structure.' Chibnall wanted this to push the boundaries of what was possible in terms of narrative and productions.

It was plotted over a few days in the summer 'in the middle of nowhere.' Early drafts had the virus make people into plastic people, but it was then probably pointed out that this has been done before (Autons). An auton line remains in the script.

As it was part of the first block a lot of the locations were filmed in South Africa standing in for Madagascar, Peru, Hong Kong. The Madagascar beach scenes were very windy (Check out Whittaker's hair in various shots) and a set blew away at one point.

Social media went berserk when the trailer showed a beach and something. Many were convinced the Sea Devils were going to make a return…sigh.

The Episode

Wow, a Doctor voice over: a rare thing. Pointless, but there we go. A spaceship is crash landing. Fast cut to a store detective preventing crime. He's not a police officer. He is getting his head straight. Then, in Chibnall style, we're in Peru. And a lot of plastic detritus ruins a beautiful river. Two girls are exploring. The tent the girls are sleeping in seems much bigger on the inside than the outside. It could be dimensionally transcendental - a Tardis even, and in this season, after the last episode, you never know. Oh, it's just badly filmed. Murmurations of birds makes this go all Hitchcock.

The failed cop gets a message from the crashing spaceman. One of the girls goes missing. Then Ryan shows up to help the girl. He's looking at dead birds

Hong Kong now. You know all of this could have been a 1970s UNIT story filmed in the home counties, right? Bradley Walsh and Yaz are there too.

Madagascar now. I mean… The Doctor is there running, finding a guy in the surf with weird stuff in his hands. He's washed up from a missing US Navy submarine. He explodes with markings over his face. Then Ryan finds the missing girl and the same thing happens.

In Hong Kong Yaz et al find the spaceman. They escape from masked bad guys. The astronaut and the ex-cop have issues. More Earth-hopping. The astronaut and the cop are/were married.

Birds are gathering. Ryan knows how to do a dissection.

The sly digs at two girls roaming and the assumption by social media stars that everyone knows them is pithy. Yaz and the Brazilian influencer teleport to a realm where the missing submarine is.

The spaceboy has the virus too.

The birds are full of plastic. The alien is in the plastic hence making the birds crazy and there's micro plastic in the water

The virus is called praxeus and we get some more Hitchcock *Birds* action but done by CGI, not with birds. It's pretty good, nevertheless

Yaz is below the Indian Ocean and under a natural pollution gyre where the virus multiplies best. Somebody has googled.

The virus is alien and it was brought by aliens to save their own planet. The antidote didn't work on the alien, but the astronaut is cured. Everyone speaks in science fiction language. Who uses the word 'comms' ever, except on tv.

The crap cop sacrifices himself in a Chibnall way, for no reason except to make him sacrifice himself.

Verdict:

Doctor Who stories about viruses have a mixed history. *The Invisible Enemy* is the most notorious (and the praxeus infection manifestation had vague stylistic similarities) but plagues (which is the more traditional name for such things) have been commonplace since Terry Nation got involved with the show. In the past the plague was usually a precursor to an invasion by a proper monster, see *The Silurians* and *Revenge of the Cybermen*. *The Invisible Enemy*'s title use of the word 'invisible' precludes that, so the virus itself was manifested ludicrously as a giant prawn at the end to general hilarity. The modern series avoids plague tales: but *The Waters of Mars* is the benchmark and quite a tough act to follow. Chibnall knows what to avoid and knew what works the solution is...

...not to have the virus manifest as a giant thing or have it as an opening salvo from an alien invasion. This is logical but stops the story having a big climax, and this story needed a big climax. He even has that idea nixed by deliberately eliminating the possibility of autons via dialogue and there would have been some of us who were disappointed the Sea Devils weren't involved after rumours spread after forensic analysis of the series trailer, where the beach was shown.

And a story where an overloaded Tardis has 6 more people to add to the plot is also going to work against it.

Plus, points we get the same director as *Spyfall* Part One, so it looks swish and globetrotting.

Therefore, this looked like it had a lot of potential. With some investigation work and a United Tardis team but it sort of frittered away into a series of set pieces which made no sense if you thought about it for a bit. Big on spectacle and little on coherence. It was merely an ok episode of Doctor Who.

As I said in the blurb above this could have been a 1970s UNIT story set in the home counties with Chibnall inflections. Having said that, it's perfectly OK in its way and this way is the way it is at the moment.

Other famous reviews:

I just don't feel *Praxeus*. A mystery with no tension, little to coo at or chuckle at, not much to chew on 2/5 - Radio Times.

Praxeus may span the planet, but the idea at the heart of this week's story isn't *quite* big enough to support the ambitious mystery it's trying to weave, leaving us with an episode that's decent but far from spectacular. Then again, *Fugitive Of The Judoon* always was going to be a tough act to follow… - Den of geek.

Once again, we are in the position of being pleasantly delighted that a story has come in at "vaguely competent" with a minimum of trauma. Even better, it's done it three stories in a row, two of them rewritten by Chibnall – Androzani.com.

Ratings: 5.22 million (4th)

Ranking: 13/24

What have we discovered? COVID makes this even scarier.

Can you Hear Me?

One Line Summary: Revisiting the vibe of the oddball stories without being odd.

Written by: Charlene James and Chris Chibnall

Charlene was an actor turned writer who did a playwright's course at the Royal Court Theatre, London. Before that she trained as ana actor at the Birmingham School of Acting. She has had several plays produced, often around issues such as mental health awareness, FGM and growing up gay in an African household. *Cutting It* was one. James cited the 8-year-old thing (again) and professed to being nervous about writing for such a wide audience.

Directed by: Emma Sullivan

In her words: she writes and directs. One of her shorts, *After Tomorrow*, was nominated for a Palme d'Or and won many awards worldwide including Best Short Film at the Edinburgh Film Festival in 2009. That year she was also named one of Screen International's Stars of Tomorrow.

Her other TV credits include *The Watch, Silent Witness, Call The Midwife*. She also claims to "have the prerequisite amount of award-winning shorts and features in development."

Anything else before we start?

Chibnall had a cancer diagnosis when he was 22. A lot of this went into Graham's character and the Doctor's weird response to him talking about it. "I think it's really important, the Doctor's reaction in that scene. I've had that numerous times. People do behave with you like that in that situation. And when people say, 'Oh I don't she'd behave like that' I go, 'People respond in really weird ways to those situations." He claims there's another cut scene where the Doctor is more sympathetic but felt the Doctor should be seen as contradictory.

Emma Sullivan got a childish desire to push every button on the set of the Tardis when she saw the set for the first time.

Charlene James wanted to cover both facing one's fears and coping with depression.

The Episode

There's always something cool about starting with an exotic location. And Aleppo in the 14th century looking stunning is a good one. Totally pointless of course, but for a while this has been the Chibnall signature and when the girl starts talking about her 'mental well-being' you realise pretty soon the setting is meaningless. Once again, this could have been set in Cardiff. I'm going to say it but, yes, the production team got all excited by world ranging titles but it's getting a bit meh now.

The girl is going on about things coming in the night. They do, and huge CGI monsters doing the *Jurassic Park* thing give us a shock.

Yaz is going to a party in Sheffield, and everyone must be back for tomorrow lunchtime.

The Doctor goes back to the Tardis, hears a snarl and a huge male face grins at the Doctor. The Tardis follows the snarl and arrives in the ruins of Aleppo after the monster attack. She finds the woman from the prologue. She says there's one still here, on the ceiling.

Yaz gets a plot line, and something is up at home. They're making something, an anniversary dinner, and catching up. Yaz sleeps and dreams of the moors. It's a bit weird. And the old man with the big face is in the room.

Ryan gets a story where we see his mate (Tibo) from the first part of *Spyfall.* Does the chips and PlayStation thing. His mate is not happy. He's finding things difficult at the moment. Tibo's been having nightmares too. The same bloke, but he has been real too. The guy's fingers detach. It's quite cool. He takes him.

Bradley Walsh gets a story and plays poker. He's having visions of a woman with grey hair but young trapped in between planets.

They all call the Doctor. The Aleppo girl, Tahira takes the Tardis's size very well. Gone are the days of people freaking out seeing it. Considering *The Dalek Master Plan* 50-years ago managed historical people not dealing with the future better, it's worrying. Here, a historical figure just talks like she's from now.

The Doctor is sure they are being targeted. She uses telepathic circuits to hone in (aka scriptal cheating).

They land on a space station. Bradley Walsh sees the two planets colliding that he saw in his dreams. They're not colliding - something between them. He sees the girl from his dreams. They also find some fingers….

The thing between the planets is a prison, the Doctor working it out in front of us. The finger guy sends them all into nightmares. Yaz's sister is rude to her in the middle of the road. Ryan is surrounded by fire and guilt trips. Bradley Walsh's cancer is back, Ruth is his nurse and she's not happy with him.

The bloke with the fingers knows the Doctor. His preferred name is Zellin. Of course, the Doctor knows the name as a mythical god. He name checks the Eternals and the Guardians and the Celestial Toymaker so the old farts go 'squeee.' He does the usual god thing and goes on about how humans are their own worst enemy.

The Doctor is fooled into freeing his partner in crime. And now there are two of them. The new god gives us a sort of PowerPoint/ You Tube clip to explain the plot via cartoon. The gods predictably decide Earth is their next target. The Doctor goes back to a dream and gets a Timeless Child hint. The monsters are all a dream, but they're used to put the gods back rather rapidly in their prison.

The fam have made friends with their close ones. Yaz has a flashback to the incident on the road. Yaz had run away. And gets some closure with the police officers who inspired her.

Bradley Walsh opens up to the Doctor about his fears of cancer returning. The Doctor is weirdly off, isn't reassuring and is frankly stupid. We have the Doctor being completely emotionally understanding about humans barely ten-minutes earlier and now isn't capable of it.

And we're off to the Villa Diodati.

Verdict:

Like the Curate's egg, there are many parts to this story. There is the haunting feeling that surrounds this and other aspects of the Chibnall era that anyone can write and make Doctor Who and you can get away with any old tat if you hit the tropes associated with Doctor Who. It's like people who go to 1970s or 1980s theme parties and just dress up in the most obviously 1980s or 1970s way possible because that's all there is. But that is just the background. You have a writer who has cut her teeth writing about mental health and so it's no surprise that we have a story devoted to mental health and people's worst fears. We have been there before of course but there is a feeling that somewhere in the mix that the original writer cares about this, a lot.

But if you burrow down into it, we have a 14th Century Syrian woman whose biggest fear is big scary alien monsters (really?). We have Yaz worried about being good enough, with a backstory that hints at bullying but doesn't go there. We have Ryan's mate (not Ryan) who has been having a tough time, which make it a bit detached and makes the whole section a little bit, 'hey kids, be like Ryan if you see someone struggling…' rather than tell a story. Then you have Graham opening up about his fear of cancer returning and the Doctor being totally weird about it and frankly being so insensitive that it almost destroys the whole point of the subtext.

The cancer scene is genuinely bizarre, so bizarre that I can't wait for when the people of this era finally talk about things (let's be honest writers history tells us this is all people will ever want to ask you about in your life's work so get your convention stories ready) who wrote this scene (We can guess and it's sort of confirmed above).

Apart from that there was no need to go to Aleppo at all, save for it being in the news a lot at the time. The namechecking of the old Who gods gives us a squee moment and some of the God-like stuff here was great. But these gods are almost identical to the ones coming up in *Flux*. It's like when the McCoy era production team didn't notice that *Remembrance of the Daleks* and *Silver Nemesis* had the same plot. The detached fingers are icky, but as ever, the baddies' plan made no sense, the Doctor's twirled her sonic. The bit where the Doctor was tied up and her sonic leapt into her hand reminded me of the terrible bad writers' trope line of 'and in one bound our hero was free,' and it was all over quickly so we could have some more emotional stuff.

It works much better as a second watch, the first time you're kind of not expecting things and you get lost. In fact, I would put it down as nearly one of my favourite Whittaker's, but it's still deeply flawed, not in direction or writing per se just in attitude and how it doesn't really get Doctor Who.

Other famous reviews:

We suspect this script started in a much better place, but after the Chibnall treatment, it's a decided fail – androzani.com.

Well, that was an odd one – Den of Geek.

A refreshingly creepy un-return to form – Daily Telegraph.

Ratings: 4.9 million (7th)

Ranking: 14/24

What have we discovered? Umm, what Aleppo used to look like.

The Haunting of Villa Diodati

One Line Summary: Because there wasn't already enough weird stuff going on at that villa that summer without adding (another) Doctor Who story.

Written by: Maxine Alderton and Chris Chibnall

Considering herself a script editor for most of her career Alderton had written 120 episodes of *Emmerdale*, with some very acclaimed ones too, including one that focussed on dementia in 2017. She's a seasoned writer and also worked on *The Worst Witch*. She feels writing Doctor Who is like soap opera writing (she is in good company as many Who writers wrote on soaps). Her favourite episode was *The Eleventh Hour* and she confessed that she preferred *Torchwood*.

Directed by: Emma Sullivan

Anything else before we start?

Just so you know what actually happened at Villa Diodati in 1816, Byron left England leaving all sorts of scandals behind him, including the fathering of his daughter Ada (Lovelace) and possible incestuous relationships with his half-sister. He rented Villa Diodati from June to November 1816. There, he met Percy Bysshe Shelley and Shelley's future wife Mary (Shelley). Also, there was John Polidori, Byron's personal physician and Mary's stepsister Claire Clairmont, who Byron was also accused of having a romantic affair with.

The weather was terrible that summer due to volcanic activity. In Indonesia Mount Tambora's eruption was the biggest in a millennium and the summer climate was a degree lower than normal. Kept in by three days of incessant rain the five started to read fantastic stories and devised their own tales. Shelley created *Frankenstein, or the modern Prometheus*, Polidori was inspired by a snippet of Byron's work to produce *The Vampyre* which would inspire all future vampire tales.

Alderton had a huge interest in the goings on of Byron and Shelley at Villa Diodati. In the true spirit of the Chibnall era what he actually said was, "she was very passionate about…something I will not tell you about." (it could be Cybermen, but we doubt it). "But she came in with that idea, that group of characters and that setting…" Alderton said this was her one shot to get into the show and it was her natural choice. She wanted the characters to equate to modern people, so Byron was a celebrity like a Kardashian

The interiors were shot in the Merthyr Mawr Estate. Lake Geneva was represented by the Llywyn Onn reservoir.

The Episode

It's 1816 on Lake Geneva and one of the most legendary evenings in literary history is taking place. There's Lord Byron, there's Mary Shelley, there's John Polidori. Percy Shelley is knocking about somewhere and in the year without a summer. They stay in and write horror stories. It's always struck me that as a Doctor Who fan these are the places where you want to go. The moment when Frankenstein AND Dracula were created. I mean, just think about that.

They're telling scary stories nicely staged and the Doctor and crew are at the door, some in historical garb except the Doctor (as usual).

Now, as I said, a story set in this period of history, in this villa is what Doctor Who should be doing…but it's already been done. *Mary's Story*, by Jonathan Morris, the 123rd Big Finish audio play went there, with a Doctor Frankenstein knocking on the door and the 8th Doctor running about as well. Obviously, they don't have to acknowledge this and probably don't even know of its existence but there's a chance that story is better. Anyway, much as Big Finish is Doctor Who because they're paid to make it this is the real stuff.

They know why they're here. "Don't mention Frankenstein (not vampires) and don't snog Byron," is glorious, form the Doctor.

And after a funny dance scene the Doctor interferes with history and suggests they write a ghost story. Hello, this is a historical, you can't interfere! She justifies it by saying they're trying to get history back on track. Shelley is missing which seems to be the problem. China is hitting the walls. And a CGI skeletal hand appear. Bradley Walsh, looking for a loo gets lost, and we realise the villa's rooms and stairs fold into each other. He's going round in circles, like Castrovalva kids.

Yaz talks to Claire about Byron's unreliability and hints at the Doctor being the same. The romance gets its first hint. Byron fancies the Doctor too, well it's certainly played that way, but Byron is clever and has seen through the Doctor's lie about their carriage having been abandoned.

Polidori is a little on edge and challenges Ryan to a dual for no real reason. Ryan gets attacked by the skeletal hand. Byron has a skeleton with his war collection. It's from there,

The Doctor gets a chance to do her best Troughton and put on a plumed hat

Shelley had seen figures visions on the lake.

The Doctor is having trouble moving round the house too. Ghosts and weird stuff abound. The house cleaner sees lights on the lake. She speaks French and we can't understand. Huh?

The Doctor has decided 'the year without a summer' was not the volcano but something arriving from another planet.

And then, at 26 minutes we see what it is, a sort of half Cyberman and this becomes something very different.
And at the same time this becomes a Doctor Who story and sort of taints the legacy of what happened in Villa Diodati because it's implied that the Cyberman inspired Shelley, as she couldn't come up with ideas without a prompt.

The Doctor is taking the cyber threat seriously. The Cyberman walks round menacingly The Doctor goes to confront the half Cyberman. Great line, "Did they get bored halfway through?" We have an emotional and angry Cyberman, which sort of isn't the point of them. The cyberium is what it's looking for. He starts quoting Shelley which is the most English literature thing ever. Yes, Shelley is the guardian. He found a weird thing in the lake, and it made him invisible. It's the knowledge and history of the Cybermen: the cyberium.

Ryan thinks Shelley should die to save millions, but the Doctor decides words matter and Shelley is incalculably important. The Doctor then gets all shirty and decides she makes the decisions and even she can't win sometimes.

It has been argued that she's defeated armies before and in other stories she could solve it with a twirl of the sonic. This legacy makes it all less dramatic despite it being played for real. Mary Shelley is nice to the Cyberman to tell his name, but he's too far gone. The cyberium leaves Shelley's body via some contrivance and it becomes a battle between the Cyberman and the Doctor. The Doctor yields under a threat to destroy the earth. What? And it all goes away

The Doctor needs to go and fix the mess she's created.

The lake they are at is not lake Geneva. Too small. And unless anyone hasn't noticed *Frankenstein* hasn't been written and nor has *The Vampyre*.

And some Byron poetry seems to be about The Doctor.

Verdict:

One of the strengths of this, in a similar way to *Rosa,* is that they got a writer in who knows a lot about the subject and gets the details right. The writer is obsessed with it, and you can see it, even if it's dropped a bit in the rewrites.

There could be the argument that in the ghettoising of education (the polymath is not encouraged, we know lots about one thing and are ignorant about the rest) is that people who become writers are only interested in literature so, is it no surprise that many of the historicals since the reboot are interested in famous authors? So, when we get a series about science things the Doctor suddenly decides 'Words Matter,' when they won't next week.

And it was nice that given the Doctor met Byron's only legitimate daughter (Ada Lovelace born six months before this was set, whom he never met) that she mentioned her to Byron. It does feel like an added scene – an afterthought.

So, it's a well-made piece of television doesn't quite work if you burrow down into it. And although nothing really makes sense, it fits in with the logic of the show. It's as if it was made by someone who had never seen Doctor Who, before. And this is fine, we want people to change the narrative but not within a season.

Having said that on first viewing I liked it a lot without any knowledge of what was to follow. The historical setting was beautifully realised and if Doctor Who was going to visit places in the past this is the sort of thing it should do but throwing away one of the most significant literary evenings in human literary history to preview a cyber story seems harsh. And to ignore the really interesting things. You have Byron and Shelley and Mary Shelley who knocked up Frankenstein and Polidori who wrote a story called the Vampyre which is the first modern take on the genre and influenced so much. It's an insane meeting of minds and it's reduced to nothing except Mary Shelley isn't writing and Byron's a bit of a shag merchant. Having said that it was creepy and funny.

Ashad's first appearance was tremendous.

This is a wasted opportunity but pretty good and it sort of trashes on the reputations of the real figures and that is a misunderstanding of what Doctor Who, but it is so well made, it gets a pass.

Other famous reviews:

Unfortunately, all this quality is in the service of a "Cybermen inspire *Frankenstein*" story. This is not so much bordering on self-parody as the capitol city. This is the sort of thing that your sixteen-year-old cousin does in a Doctor Who fanfic you go, "oh, bless." It's an idea that when Big Finish did, everyone went "well that's a bit obvious, isn't it?" It's the most tedious, unimaginative "going with your first idea" bit of bullshit the series has coughed up in recent memory—an idea that is not merely bad but insulting - Tardis Eruditorium.

An episode that's well written, well-acted and actually entertaining has become an endangered species. We're massively grateful just to spot one in the wild – Androzani.com.

The Haunting of Villa Diodati comes together as more than the sum of its ill-fitting parts - Den of Geek.

Ratings: 5.07 million (7th)

Ranking: 9/24

What have we discovered? A slightly wasted opportunity.

Ascension of the Cybermen/The Timeless Children

One Line Summary: Oh right, Ok. Are you sure about this?

Written by: Chris Chibnall

Directed by: Jamie Magnus Stone

Anything else before we start?

The Timeless Child twist was planned from Chibnall's earliest pitch meetings with the BBC. It was mentioned in *The Ghost Monument,* therefore it's likely. "When people were having opinions about the first female Doctor, I thought 'well this is going to be interesting, because we haven't even started yet!'"

He elaborated on his plans: "I knew from the start. And it was part of what I talked to Charlotte [Moore] and Piers [Wenger] about, just opening up the mythology to more stories. The purpose was to bring narrative opportunity and to be able to go to places that were shut off before now. That's the big thing really."

Later he said with relation to his successor:" It's one of the few drama series without a written bible, and every era contains a contradiction or left turn from what has come before. Any future showrunner will ignore it or run with it... Oh, I fully expect Russell to ignore it!"

The Cybermen didn't return in Season 11 because of their huge input into Season 11.

And for those who are counting Bradley Walsh claimed this was his favourite episode "By a country mile." Yes, I know he also said that about *Rosa*.

The Episodes

Ascension of the Cybermen

A voice over from Ashad, the partly converted Cyberman about how empires can rise again is so squee you can't wait, but deep down, you just know they'll mess it up.

Then, in the modern way, we cut to a rural Irish setting and a baby is discovered. Now at the time this was weird but quite good. Now we know it as an allegory. Brendan, the baby is adopted, and we see happy rurality. It ends with 'if it gets worse, I'll call the Doctor.'

The Doctor and fam are on Shelley's coordinates in what looks like a Welsh village augmented with CGI (ha ha, has the budget run out? It's Prosser farm in Brecon). The cyber wars have left only seven humans alive. Really? And they're the usual rag bag bunch of slightly earnest hippies talking in serious ways.

The Doctor has weapons, and one makes the Cybermen realise how much pain they are in. Do they have nerves suddenly? I suppose it's better than gold. When the Cybermen were allowed to be taken the piss out of (around 1985) whole lists of things were drawn up of all the things 'the impossible to defeat' Cybermen were vulnerable too. Yaz has a machine that spits gold dust into the air. Because 'the Cybermen are allergic to gold, right?'

Cyberheads - sorry drones CGI their way over. Fantastically, all the weapons are useless, which makes me very happy. We get stunt somersaults from extras, like the UNIT era but it's a bad day for the Doctor. And the humans grudgingly obey her. She's fantastically stroppy here and takes the fam out of the equation. She sends them away. The Doctor goes to confront Ashad. The humans escape without Ryan. It's a fantastic start, however, the Tardis being out of the game by being 'too far away' is a bit limp. The Doctor, Ryan and a token human steal a cyber ship

Then we're back to Ireland and the boy becomes a police officer.

Back at the cyber wars and it becomes a bit Sawardian in dialogue style (tough and futuristic). The Doctor has a ding dong with Ashad, and he hints at the death of everything.

In Ireland we have a cliff edge and a gun. Boom and our man falls. Not dead and that's weird.

Yaz is doing her stare into space and think about the Doctor thing. Bradley Walsh playing a pensioner from Sheffield tells seasoned veterans from a future beset by fear how to solve space problems. And then he reads some lines out. They end up on a cyber ship. Yaz is proud of him, unfortunately the ship is a cyber troop carrier.

The Doctor does some stuff and finds someone called Ko Sharmus aka that Barristan Selmy from *Game of Thrones*, and who the Doctor thinks it's a planet. He helped everyone escape through 'the barrier.' It's in the sea.

Ashad, the cyber hybrid has boarded, and the troop shop contains old Cybermen. Love them. But Ashad is making them scream. We get old-school Cybermen waking up.

The police officer is now old and retiring. Gets a clock. And the end it goes all weird and the people from the story attach electrodes and wipe his mind.

Gallifrey is through Ko Sharmus's barrier, and the Master shows up.

The Timeless Children

The Master is all serious as the Doctor goes through to Gallifrey. The cyber ship arrives with the rest of the Cybes and Chibnall gets bored of characters he can't be bothered with anymore. Bradley Walsh thinks they can disguise themselves in cyber casings. Right, it's an effective scene and the director plays up to it with shots through the cyber eye casings. Yet, they're all through the mesh of the costume. Do actual Cybermen have such poor vision? Do they look through the mesh of the costume? Clearly not. Are Cybermen hollow? No! So, it is stupid.

The Doctor is a bit limp with the Master. They're in the ruined Panopticon and the Master invites the Cybermen in as well.

Bradley Walsh and Yaz have a talkie bit before the action. It's a bit weird.

The Master sends the Doctor into the Matrix to find the truth. She sees the world of Tecteun, the traveller who found a gateway and a timeless child thrown through from the realm. It's a child who regenerates. Are you getting this?

The Cybermen arrive, Ryan does a basketball shot and kills loads. Ashad meets the Master, the Cybermen have a death particle. And you get the feeling (again) that Chibnall gets bored of his own stories. he ruins a perfectly good story set in the Villa Diodati with a BRILLIANT cyber thing and then the story about the BRILLIANT cyber thing is ruined by making the Master own him. I suspect Chibnall regrets this and doesn't realise that Ashad is a monumentally good creation. He will regret that.

The Master is all serious and the Doctor goes through to Gallifrey. The cyber ship arrives with the rest of the cast.

Ashad meets the Master. The Cybermen have a death particle. Chibnall clearly gets bored with his stories, so

The child regenerates lots and is used to feed the regeneration programme on Gallifrey. Of course, the kid is the Doctor!! The rest is history as the Master does classic acting stance and look into the distance.

Meanwhile, Cybermen attack Ryan's group and of course irritatingly the Cybermen are vulnerable to these weapons for plot convenience but weren't to similar weapons in the previous episode. Then the Cybes are attacked by other Cybes who are actually Yaz and Graham. I mean I know Ian pretended to be a Dalek in *The Daleks* in 1964 but it was 1964. How likely is this? Yaz would have been a tiny Cyberman, not the giant shown here.

The Master has heard a lot about the cyberium 'over the millennia.' Well, how come the viewers who've seen a few Cybermen stories haven't? Yes, there's some guff about this being in the far future but it seems rather convenient. And then Ashad is TCE[7]'d just like that and the cyberium is a mercury ball. The Master then seems annoyed that the death particle didn't destroy everything when Ashad was miniaturised. What a waste of a fine character. The Master hosts the cyberium and it hurts. The Doctor and the Master stand by an Ordnance Survey trig point on a hill. Glad to see trig points are common in the universe. Do the production team know what it is? Nope.

The Division was created as a sort of force for bad within the politics of Time Lords. There are gaps and it's suggested that the Doctor's involvement in the Division has been redacted and the Irish bits are legacy memories etc.

Suddenly, all this is put on the back burner as we have new Cybermen time Lord mash ups - Cybes with time Lord hats. Cyberlords.

The fam and hangers-on arrive on Gallifrey to rescue the Doctor (you can guess which four are likely to die). The other (Jo Martin) Doctor arrives, gives our Doctor a cryptic pep talk and the Doctor rallies and breaks out of the Matrix by drawing up memories including the 'you know what' scene from the *Brain of Morbius,* although only for a second.

---

[7] Tissue Compression Eliminator

The way out is a Pertwee-like explosion, but the teeny death particle seeded before can eliminate all of this before it was really a threat.

Oh, and the other way out is that the Doctor must set off the bomb and must sacrifice herself but of course she's just found out she's immortal, so it's hardly drama. As the final confrontation with the Master happens the Doctor admits this in more flowery language. I mean to threaten to blow everything up when everyone can regenerate…

But don't worry Ko Sharmus is here to save the day in the usual Chibnallian self-sacrifice, while the Master and the cyber lords just hang around waiting.

The fam get home in a spare Tardis disguised as a house (unintentionally hilarious) and the Doctor is caught by the Judoon.

Verdict:

It has been easy to criticise the 13th Doctor's era but I'm going to say it: *Ascension of the Cybermen* and *The Timeless Child* are very well-made pieces of television. The scripts are polished and move from one place to another, with intriguing set pieces. The effects and direction are fine. To a producer or manager, it looks great and does what Doctor Who does. It will even manage to get lots of 'wows' from social media in the aftermath.

And if you expect me to say 'not!' after all this praise then you are wrong. It *is* all these things. It's just none of these things are necessarily what makes Doctor Who great.

It's been mentioned before and is legendary how Jean-Marc L'Officier reviewed *The Deadly Assassin*, with the overly hysterical 'what has happened to the magic of Doctor Who?' and sometimes I wonder what I would have felt had I watched that episode live back in the day. I don't need to wonder; I know I would have hated it. However, we now know that it is one of the greatest pieces of Doctor Who ever.

So, I would have been wrong, and I would like to argue that this could be the same for the future. The problem here is of course that *The Deadly Assassin* had huge viewing figures, and everyone had given up on this. Nobody cared.

Part of the reason is because the beats of the programme are the same each week. We know there will be a noble human sacrifice, the baddies all speak the same way. The structure (I say it again), written for intelligent 8-year-olds, with blah blah blah, with added comedy beats like Davies and Moffat used to do without either of their genius.

I don't quite have a problem with the Doctor being the timeless child and having a huge gap in her life where she was some kind of secret agent, and she is the most important Time Lord ever and she's not even a Time Lord: I just don't think the show needed it.

And destroying a brilliant character like Ashad for the sake of the Master?

So, this is it; this is where you start to wonder whether Doctor Who is done. That for a show with infinite possibilities has in fact exhausted all its possibilities and there is nothing left to say. I think it has and that makes me sad.

Other famous reviews:

Ascension Of The Cybermen is a long way from perfect. Luckily for it, it's got some good parts, and it benefits from being the first half of the story. As a result, it's a pretty fun watch - Androzani.com.

But then after *The Timeless Children…*

We're tired of the gasping. We're tired of the monotonous pace and inflection of the delivery. We're tired of the embarrassing bragging swiftly followed by ignominious failure. We're tired of her resorting to the sonic screwdriver in every single situation. We're tired of villains pushing her around and her letting them. We're tired of the utter absence of conveying that she's an alien with many long lives behind her. As a result, whether she's a mysterious regenerating being from another realm or a small tree frog, we can't really bring ourselves to care – Androzani.com.

Could this episode have ever lived up to its own hype? Probably not. Had *Fugitive of the Judoon* not existed we'd all be left reeling from the surprise – Den of Geek.

What an awful, boring mess. That's what I jotted in my notebook halfway through this Doctor Who finale and it didn't much improve. The Doctor needs a long rest – Patrick Mulkern (Radio Times).

Ratings: 4.69 million (30th in the week) the lowest rated episode since the last low (*Eaters of Light*). There are more to come.

Ranking: 6/24

What have we discovered? Yes, they can complete destroy established continuity but, in the process, also destroy viewing figures.

Revolution of the Daleks

One Line Summary: Captain Jack and the pointless waste of time.

Written by: Chris Chibnall

Directed by: Lee Haven Jones

Anything else before we start?

Early drafts had the AI defence drones rolled out in Russia, killing off lots of World Leaders and taking over Earth.

John Barrowman got his last BBC credit before being blacklisted for allegations of sexual misconduct on set. His return had been planned 'for a long time' and, as is the way with this era, there were lots of 'secret meetings,' Chibnall was smuggled backstage to a concert once. Barrowman had a flat in Cardiff still and had the excuse ready, that he was remodelling it. Captain Jack's return was always pencilled in.

Director Lee-Haven Jones "did a lot of work trawling through past Dalek episodes to learn from the past to identify when the Daleks were at their scariest." He was particularly proud to have even watched some of the black and white ones. Not surprisingly, he came up with exactly the same conclusion legendary Classic Era director Graeme Harper did in 1984 when he was asked to direct Daleks for the first time: "shooting a Dalek from below and close up gives it a very forbidding look."

The key confrontation scene of Bristol's iconic Clifton suspension bridge was Haven-Jones' favourite scene. It was covered up by an advance notice that the bridge would be shut overnight 'for an inspection.' "The Trust is reviewing its access requirements to the main chain anchorage to determine if they can be improved. These accesses are in the middle of the bridge and therefore any inspection needs to be carried during a road closure." They did not close the bridge to pedestrians, so many fans got a sneak preview.

The Episode

It starts with a *Star Wars* 'long time ago' thing, which isn't funny and less funny when they caveat that's its Cheltenham in 2019. It's GCHQ, a Dalek, the Doctor, and the fam zapping it and it's from *Resolution*, of course.

367 minutes later (um, see previous comments about how many tone meeting came up with that number) and workers get rid of the remains of the Dalek. The driver is taken out by a roadside cafe and the Dalek is stolen. It's a bit random.

Mr Big from *Arachnids*, is back, with a politician and a geek. They demonstrate a riot clearing device that is of course…come on, a proper Dalek. Everyone laughs at it, but it has built in water cannon, cs gas and sonic deterrent. The politician is keen.

The Doctor is in space prison and has been stuck there for ages. But as noted a million times before, in other stories she would be out in a minute. There are Ood, P'ting, and Angel inmates. She's quoting Harry Potter.

Ryan and Graham are at the house Tardis from the last story. Yaz is there. It's in a different place to the last story, but never mind. It's been ten-months, only Yaz gives a damn, and we know why. But Ryan and Graham have seen the Dalek and Mr Big on the TV.

The politician is now PM and the fam find Mr Big. The fam fail to get to him to stop his Dalek research.

Captain Jack breaks the Doctor out of prison, and she bitches about plastic surgery. It took Jack 19-years to get her: a bit Moffatian. The Doctor is back in the Tardis, saying she was, 'in prison for being me just when I wasn't sure who I was.' She says it was decades. It's difficult to show decades on a female Doctor. A male actor would just grow a beard, so it's unconvincing, though no-one's fault.

The geek (Leo) working for Mr Big is nervous and has grown a Dalek from cellular remnants. Mr Big pretends to be outraged and uses the line, 'this is why people don't like experts.' Ooh, paraphrase Michael Gove: that's satire. Leo tries to incinerate the Dalek, but it wasn't having any of it and now he's possessed by it.

The Doctor goes back to the fam. Really, after decades? And then we get emotional scene about it being ten-months for them, it's just to have the scene.

In Japan, the possessed Leo is in a lab making more Daleks.

Captain Jack tried to explain his backstory, but it seems like from another world and it doesn't work quite as well as it did in our heads.

The Doctor goes to see Mr Big and his Dalek casings. He thinks he's 3D printing security drones.

Captain Jack says he's from the 51st century and Yaz seems astonished. Yaz, how long have you been travelling in time? This should be totally normal.

Now we get the Yaz/Doctor romance thing, and we get Jack explain the wonder of 'being there.' "Being with the Doctor you don't get to choose when it stops." I think there was scope to work on this using Ryan, who doesn't seem to care and Yaz who really cares, who really gets it but this conversation in the middle of a Dalek crisis? It's a Chibnall trope to do this, btw: talkie bits at the wrong moment, and it never works, not once.

The Prime Minister has her Daleks, sorry defence drones.

Now Ryan and the Doctor have a heart to heart. And Ryan is clearly going to leave. It's weird how unbothered he is. That might be the case but why did the Doctor take him with her?

The Daleks get in the casings and start killing people. It's so … unscary.

The Prime Minister gets zapped. Leo gets zapped.

The Doctor says, 'I'm the Doctor,' but all she has is the nuclear option, which is bring in proper Daleks: sounds like *Resurrection of the Daleks* again. The Daleks zap each other and, as usual, the battle is horrifically static. Robinson does the stupid thing. As usual it's all sorted out quite quickly

A massive bomb and trapping the Daleks in the Master's Tardis that the Doctor has programmed to destroy solves the problem here.

Jack Robertson survives again. Ryan and Graham don't want to go to the meringue galaxy. Can't the characters or the creators not appreciate it's a time machine? You can go and come back, and no time has gone. You can be with the Doctor and open your mind to a universe of brilliance.

Verdict:

Another similar adventure that riffs off so much from the past, with absolutely no idea of a new direction. The old clichés about Doctor Who, about how it was filmed stagey, in a studio, meant imagination and words became key and now it is never about words, or ideas, just repackaging what has happened from misremembered good bits. Like a 1980s theme party that makes everyone dress up in grotesque parodies of fleeting fashions from a 10-year period and people dance to the same records that have been curated to mean the 1980s. Now Doctor Who has become its own theme party, where the stories ape accepted old ones, the companions do what companions do and even the Doctor doesn't really change. We will never see another *Kinda, Warrior's Gate, Ribos Operation*. You just see riffs off accepted Dalek stories, *The Deadly Assassin* and post 2005 hits. There weren't even any good bits, even Captain Jack who can usually liven up anything, is flat and pointless. The narrative makes no sense, even if the plot does but even with 80-minutes (which was the running time of a 4-parter in the old days) this fails to tell a suspenseful story.

Other famous reviews:

So, what do you get if you show someone *Revolution of the Daleks*? What sort of show will they conclude that Doctor Who is? An aging franchise with its interests firmly rooted in the past, with little to offer save for past glories - Elizabeth Sandifer.

This is unlikely to be anyone's all-time favourite Doctor Who episode. It won't sit proudly in the number one spot when YouTubers rank the Christmas specials. It's a little too reliant on navel-gazing for that – but what the episode does is try and tackle questions raised by the Doctor always being the centre of the series' universe, and what it takes to overcome her gravitational pull. Even if you don't care to chew over those metatextual issues on New Year's Day, however, *Revolution of the Daleks* is still an enjoyable hour-and-change of telly, and one that ultimately chooses to (mostly) wipe the slate clean ready for adventures yet to come - Den of Geek.

Doctor Who has always been mediocre, and we've only just noticed. - brainofmorbius.com.

Ratings: 6.25 million (10th)

Ranking: 19/24

What have we discovered? A real sense of utter despair.

Season 13

Flux

One Line Summary: The Covid season

New Cast: John Bishop

Born in Liverpool in 1966 he was a semi-pro football player before going into medical sales. His side hustle of stand-up comedian led to TV work and thoughtful presentation gigs. He had done occasional acting work but Doctor Who was the biggest deal, by far.

Written by: Chris Chibnall (1-6), Maxine Alderton (4)

Directed by: Jamie Magnus Stone (1,2,4)

Azhur Saleem (3,5,6)
He calls himself a lazy animator who picked up a camcorder. Started as a runner and moved onto music videos. A graduate of the London Film School, he took the path of many new directors by writing and producing his own short films in order to showcase and hone his directorial skills. And the results certainly highlight him as a name to watch out for. They included *Muse*, available as part of the *Dust* YouTube channel. He went on to direct Neil Gaiman's *The Anansi Boys* and did second unit Direction stuff for *War of the Sontarans*.

He hadn't really watched 'the old stuff'; and went to Matt Smith stories for inspiration, thinking, "it's not where we are now in terms of set design."

Anything else before we start?

This is the story that nearly never got made because of the restrictions related to COVID were immense. According to Chibnall they could only make one 6-part rolling narrative story because of restrictions related to set building. Chibnall felt it was a miracle that it was made at all, which sounds like getting his excuses in early.

Also, interior location filming was avoided because of COVID restrictions of numbers in small spaces. Chibnall cites the Scandi house on *The Halloween Invasion* as a rare example and irritating to shoot.

Sarah Powell (Mary Seacole) "The cast and crew: indoors, outdoors, in winter, in Wales in the rain and mud, everyone wearing masks and being tested every 5 minutes: I loved stepping onto their ship and riding with them for a while."

War of the Sontarans kept getting rained off. We know that a lot of who was kept secret but the quarry where this was filmed was definitely in the Brecon Beacons because Peter McTighe says he saw them when they were filing his series *The Pact* in the woods over the road: Morlais quarry.

Once, Upon Time was always supposed to be a 'Mad, out there episode.'

For *Once Upon Time* the film *Cloud Atlas* was an inspiration and producer Matt Strevens felt Haleem's short film *Artichoke* – had similar vibes.

The real problem was time, as costume, make-up, and hair to be done at various times rather than at the same time.

According to Danny Marie Elias the designer Karvanista's design was based on Chibnall's dog, but the designer had a Staffy and some of that came in, along with some Samurai facial hair. Swarm and Azure were given an almost anime feel, as if they were fantasy world creatures. Their androgyny was also important, blue for Azure and pink for the male Swarm.

"Journey," the PS game inspired the giant Passenger concept.

The Episodes

Note: I am considering *Flux* as a whole, semi-reluctantly, but will give each episode a min-review and tidy everything up at the end.

Similarly, and the creators might have thought of this too, it might be useful to explain exactly what the Flux is before we get started. It is a cataclysmic event designed to destroy the universe and made from anti-matter originating from outside the universe. It was created by The Division, who under Techteun had decided to abandon this universe for another one. All the chaos that lies ahead is because of this.

The Halloween Apocalypse

Scene 1

The opening scene was an obvious 'here's the new season with the Doctor and Yaz in peril' shot but the dialogue is so obvious, and nobody really takes it seriously. There's a point where a CGI background and a threat based on other computer-generated things becomes pointless and when you hear the baddie talking about planet Earth you think, did a fourteen-year-old write this, especially as there is no threat? This is the opening scene of a show that is haemorrhaging viewers, you know. It's not even resolved cleverly except for the two female characters to end up landing on a bed. And it takes less than a second to think that: "isn't that just to stoke things in the will they won't they scenario but in a PG way?" Since when has there been a bed in the console room?

Karvanista is mentioned though, a supposedly super important person. You know, (as we'll see) who worked with the Jo Martin Doctor in the Division and is the only other survivor of that time. The Doctor and Yaz (in Yaz's case unknowingly) track him down to find secrets of the Doctor's past. You might have missed that the way this scene was set up which comes across as a grumpy Mancunian voice overdubbed onto the CGI action.

Scene 2: A very tightly shot set in Liverpool in 1820, which tells us nothing except something big is going on. The tunnel builder is one Joseph Williamson, a real-life philanthropist who did build a load of tunnels in the Edge Hill area of Liverpool. The reasons he did so were unclear and I'm sure Chibnall won't mind clearing it up for us with a Doctor Who explanation.

Scene 3: We get John Bishop as Dan, a sort of Walter Mitty like character working but not working as a museum guide.

Scene 4: Another explanation scene as the Swarm is seen incarcerated, it's clearly about to be released. And this is the problem with this era: nothing flows. In the *Sea Devils* in 1972 they could do a better 'there's a bad guy incarcerated but he's clearly got the upper hand on the guards' scene? Swarm has what is known as a Lon Cheney nose, or if you prefer, a 'local people' *League of Gentlemen* (the British version) nose. He knows the Doctor.

Scene 5: Back in the Tardis COVID restrictions mean that every scene has effectively been a two header so far.

Scene 6: Dan is at a food bank. Political. Dan lives near Anfield, probably to remind us that we're in Liverpool. Dan is lonely and alone and the director does a *Breaking*

Bad back of fridge perspective shot. Then Karvanista arrives and he's a giant dog with a northern accent. It doesn't work. It's played for laughs. The Tardis arrives. The Doctor was a ball boy for 'Trent' once and saw the Barcelona match nine times. The Doctor quite clearly didn't do this. On the trail of Karvanista they find out seven billion Lupari ships are headed to Earth. The house is shrunk in a Karvanista trap.

Scene 7 In the Arctic a couple find a thing in their shed. The woman smashes it. But it makes no difference.

Scene 8 Dan is in space and gets no answer from Karvanista about why.

Scene 9 Yaz gets no answers from the Doctor either about why she's obsessed with Karvanista. I'm not sure people care. A woman comes up who knows them. She's Claire, she'll be important.

Scene 10: The Tardis is being weird; the Doctor is being weird.

Scene 11 Claire encounters a weeping angel. She knows not to blink she gets zapped into the past.

Scene 12: Grey Worm from *Game of Thrones,* sorry, new character Vinder, does his Lister from *Red Dwarf* Shtick. Alone on Observation Planet Rose. Nothing is happening and then something happens. As planets burn, he leaves his post.

Scene 13: Arctic Circle - our ugly friend (Swarm) comes to get his sister (Azure) who was disguised as the woman. Why?

Scene 14: The Doctor and Yaz are on Karvanista's ship, which Karvanista calls a spaceship. Because we call ships sea ships. My friend Andy would like that though it channels the memory of Terry Nation where the word 'space' could be put in front of anything to make it sound cool. The writing has got sloppy here. They're bickering. It's what happens when you have two characters saying lines and you think you're being funny. They think they're writing *Some Like it Hot,* but it never is like *Some Like it Hot*. Karvanista says that the Earth festival Halloween might cause some operational problems. Really?

Right, so Karvanista knows about the Division yet the casual viewer (and there weren't many of them) is supposed to remember this from 18-months before, with no recap at all. Then Karvanista in his role as plot exposition explains that (ludicrously) his people have a human each to save from the Flux which is coming this way. Hence Dan is on his ship because that's his human. Dan's line about a mate having a Tardis but his was bigger was glorious - classic scouse humour.

And then the Sontarans turn up as well.

The Tardis takes them to see the flux and rings the cloister bell. The Doctor has another psychic link with Swarm but has no recollection.

Diane waits for her date with Dan date by a random scary house - in Liverpool. She's got by Azure. What are the chances and why?

The Flux engulfs the Tardis, and the cliff-hanger is a reminder of who we've met in this episode.

Mini Review

This is tough to review. In some ways any criticisms of modern Doctor Who are clearly seen here. Overly CGI'd, too many characters, plot exposition done at a high pace, nobody was sure what was going on.

No long-term fan could ever have had much to say about the companion dynamic for thirteen. It just didn't work and there were pleas for Yaz to get a chance to be the solo companion. Well, we got what we wanted and it's, sort of OK. The opening scene is cute, if still childish in its execution and had absolutely zero peril because of it. I'm giving it a pass.

The other criticism ('observation' is better) is that in a world of Netflix and other streamed ten-part arc stories it seemed strange that the original long story show had stuck with squeezing all the action into one 45-minute episode. Wouldn't it be great to go for a long arc? Well, we've got it with *Flux* and therefore it is difficult to judge this as a single episode. It's here to set a scene. The trouble is it didn't do it very well.

Doctor Who was always theatre-style sci fi. Character driven, a few sets, innovative design. They are its roots. It is not space opera and whenever it tries it struggles. And now the BBC can clearly do a billion spaceships and any alien landscape you like, you are left with a show that looks like everything else.

So, an attempt at a sort of Netflix-style long series is welcome, but it fails spectacularly at the first hurdle. The premiere episode of a long series must be gripping, where this was confusing, with explanation mumbled under music and noise. Any continuity needed must be given to casual viewers, with a 'previously on.' What we get are lots of threads added to an existing arc and making it confusing. Also, Chibnall baddies are always the same. Swarm could be Tim Shaw or those immortals from *Can You Hear Me*?

Yes, yes it was filmed under COVID restrictions. You can see it if you know where to look, with almost every scene a two-hander, or cleverly shot.

The Sontarans being back is always welcome but Angels too? There is too much going on and the tone is all off. Again, Whittaker's Doctor flits between a ball of energy that is wrong for this story and someone not assertive enough. The general consensus is that they tried to add too much to the first episode, paring back the introduction of Vinder and perhaps the tunnels guy to later episodes might have helped.

And Karvanista is a dog, and it is silly. Yes, Chewbacca worked in 1978, but Dorf from *Mindwarp* was a better realised canine alien and that was 40-years ago.

We start with a weird black and white opening explained by the Doctor and a house that isn't.

The Doctor is then in a Cold War zone. Corpses in British uniforms; Mary Seacole comes and tells them off for being looters. Her accent is very Caribbean. It's the Crimean war 1855. The Doctor asks about Russians and Seacole looks confused. They're not fighting Russians they're fighting Sontarans. Now if you watch Doctor Who for the 'good bits,' the things no other show can do then this reveal and the sight of a Sontaran on a horse is for you.

Then (again) the story loses the momentum by focussing on Vinder and an upturned pyramid (a priest triangle) who asks, 'can you repair?' There are some sleeping women like statues. These are the Mouri.

Back to Crimea, Mary Seacole is presented well and sympathetically, and someone has done the research. Dan disappears in blue smoke, so does Yaz. The Doctor can't get in the Tardis (no door), and all this distracts us from the usual crap about history being changed which only ever works on Earth.

Dan is back in a deserted Liverpool. Huge Sontaran ships are above Liverpool and chase him (they can't aim as usual) and his mum and dad can beat Sontarans with saucepans bashed on the probic vent. Not helping the serious tone this.

Yaz is in the place where Vinder was and the bloke from the tunnels in the previous episode (Joseph Williamson) appears. He's from 1820. 'Can you repair?'

asks a pyramid again? Yaz, rather cutely, has WWTDD written on her hand. We could ask when she wrote that, but we'll be nice.

Back in Crimea and the Doctor has a frank and fair discussion with an army general and sees that Sontar is on the map, not Russia and China. It's great moment. Seacole is also treating a Sontaran which gives Dan Starkey (ex-Strax) a chance to do his Sontaran turn. They let him go and he leads them to the Sontaran forces. The Crimea looks very wet (not sure that's historically accurate (but they get the uniforms right!) The Doctor puts Seacole on monitoring duty of the huge Sontaran camp.

Yaz and Vinder meet in the temple of Atropos and have a talkie bit. The triangles are priests on the planet Time and all time must pass through the Mouri who the women on pedestals are. Got that?

Dan is watching Sontarans dealing with captured humans. It reminds me a bit of *Dalek Invasion of Earth* but for some reason it's not as powerful. I think it's because you showed ordinary people dealing with Sontarans with saucepans earlier.

The Doctor has a parley with a Sontaran called Skaak, who name-drops Linx from *The Time Warrior*. I thought they were clones? The Sontarans used the Lupari shield to invade Earth.

The British overrule the Doctor after attempts at diplomacy seem to work. There's a huge CGI battle which nearly fools you. Sorry, I mean massacre. The Doctor and Mary get on a Sontaran ship and now a catapult will kill the Sontarans. They meet Dan via a time thing. The plot is revealed, the Sontarans want to take over all Earth history and the Doctor instructs Dan to stop it. He does the frying pan thing again and then Karvanista saves him.

Swarm and Azure turn up with a silent partner called The Passenger. Azure kills off the triangles. They banter with Yaz and Vinder and prove unkillable (in part 2, but don't worry).

The Doctor aims to attack the Sontarans on their rest cycle. Chibnall is obsessed by the probic vent and seems to imply it's only on Earth like planets that it's needed. It all sorts itself out. They all go from time and the Doctor gets Dan back.

The Tardis is hijacked, and all the spatial readings are at zero. They're on the planet Time and Yaz is now a Mouri, as is Vinder and the full force of time is about to go blast through them. The Doctor begs Swarm, but he doesn't care.

Mini Review

Undoubtedly the most watchable of the season, the Sontarans are always worth watching and the alternate history is done well. The other bits hint at a bigger picture and the COVID restrictions are less obvious, or as it's more watchable perhaps you notice less. This was clearly written as a stand-alone and dropped into the mix once it was decided to go with the Flux storyline. It doesn't work because of it although the Sontaran story does look quite wonderful. It's a shame it wasn't made in that form.

Already the cracks in the flux framework are showing. Has the universe collapsed, or hasn't it?

And now we have a complete curveball, with Bel's story. I don't think Flux as story needed this. Bel avoids Daleks in a ruined woodland world and talks to an unnamed loved one on a device. Survivors of the Flux are being zapped by murmurations of blue particles.

Then it's back to the Doctor, who retrofits the action from the cliffhanger and falls into a void. She has literally bought time; her friends all zap off into the universe. And an angel is there too.

Be warned, this is messy. This is a holding episode before the Angels arrive and the Doctor is revealed to have a part in existence of the flux.

The Doctor and team are talking in sci fi 'butch' military tones, with weapons, blatantly in a studio. That's a bit random. It's not clear on first viewing that it's people we know being other people we don't know, so it's simply weird. They're on Atropos and the Doctor sees the renegade Doctor in a mirror. So, is this a lost Doctor memory? And is one of them Karvanista then? Couldn't he have played himself?

Dan has a domestic Liverpool scene with his girlfriend Di, but the scene is broken up by the blue murmurations. The time frames are deliberately messy. The Passenger watches by the catholic cathedral in Liverpool. Dan ends up in the weird tunnels with the old Joseph Williamson. It's in Edge Hill. Dan says he's from there. Wasn't his house by Anfield?

Yaz is back in the police and the Doctor is also a police officer and then isn't. An angel is in the wing mirror.

Vinder and Yaz are in the future on his planet and Vinder sees through the illusion because he doesn't want to have these memories. But this has meaning as the Grand Serpent is introduced, as Vinder is to work for him.

Bel returns. Look there are just too Many threads. Do we need the Cybermen too?

Now, the Grand Serpent is played by Craig Parkinson and is an excellent choice. No ambiguity that he is evil and of course he's called the Grand Serpent.

Yaz and her sister. Too much!! More Angels in the computer game.

The Doctor is back in her Division time meeting Swarm and Azure. The Passenger is a long-forbidden form, a holding entity that can store what it captures a living prison with endless capacity (remember that).

Is the substitution of characters a COVID thing?

Bel is now on a Lupari spaceship and Dan kills a legion of Cybermen. Love is the only mission.

The Grand Serpent is being evil and during a routine meeting asks Vinder to stop the recording even though his words to stop the recording will be recorded. Vinder does the right thing and pays the price.

The Mouri throw the Doctor out and then she meets an old woman Awsok, who tells her the universe is over. The flux was made and it's the Doctor's fault and she's sent back to the actual present. Swarm is so busy trying to destroy the universe but has time to steal Dan's girlfriend and put her in a Passenger. For god's sake

And of course, Bel is Vinder's girlfriend. Vinder is looking for her too.

And now the Angels arrive.

Mini Review

Everyone knows this is an absolute mess. For the average viewer it's confusing as to what is real and what isn't. We have past Doctor stuff of real importance to the plot while Yaz is playing computer games with her sister. The Doctor stuff is so important but it's unclear because the Doctor is in the time from the Division era but played by Whittaker, when Jo Martin would have been the better choice and Dan and Vinder are there playing other people. One of the other problems is that it is never clear on first viewing who is important and who isn't. Take Dan's relatives who we met last episode, are we seeing them again? What does Bel bring to the plot?

A coherently set up in the last episode with Jo Martin playing the Doctor now would have helped, but who needs the rest?

As the Independent said: "The viewer, meanwhile, is left banging their head against a wall as they try to figure out what's actually important and what's never going to come up again."

Village of the Angels

It's 1967 Claire, the woman from the first episode is there telling the truth about being born in 1985. She's in distress and says to an old Hugo Lang (that's a *Twin Dilemma joke* kids). She has some kind of fit and says, 'the angel has the Tardis.' Which, after the opening titles, is true. Now I'm a fan of the Angels, certainly in *Blink* and the *Time of Angels,* but after a while, they can't sustain the suspense, but you always live in hope.

The Doctor escapes the Angel that's invaded the Tardis and lands in 1967. The whole village is looking for a little girl. The bit where she sniffs the old man's coat to work out it's 1949, only to be told it's 1967, followed by, 'you've had that coat a long time,' is glorious. It's good to see the Doctor in the past but not in that pious 'don't change history' vibe; it's as if they've forgotten about it. It's also worth praising the mickey taking of management speak that is another hallmark of this era. The 'flat team structure' line being the fine example here.

The Doctor meets Claire and likes Jericho's (not Hugo Lang) first name (Eustacius). Claire has angel wings when she looks in the mirror. The vicar is counting graves and finds an angel and is zapped.

Dan and Yaz search for the girl. There are weird lights but it's Angel-related. Yaz says 'don't blink' but does - a lot. They get zapped into the past.

Now we're back to Bel. I know, let's spoil a good story by taking us out of it. She's on Puzano the only planetary remaining in the 'quadrant' and a staging place for those who have survived the Flux event.

Jericho has Angels surrounding his house. It's a well-done scene. Claire does her back story and tells the Doctor that everyone disappears in the village tonight, just as they did in 1901. The Doctor says time isn't always fixed. But it's an Earth in the past story Doctor, therefore it is - usually. Consistency guys!

Dan and Yaz are in an empty 1901, sent there by the Angels. looking for the missing girl. It's empty except for a record player that is not from 1901. The missing girl is here and says the Angels are responsible. You can't escape out of the village, and it seems to be stuck in space.

In 1967 the Angels stalk the house and Claire reveals she's an angel or harbouring one. The Doctor mind melds with her, and we go all black and white Ingmar Bergman. The Angel needs her help. It's a rogue angel and the Angels work for The Division.

Back with Bel and Azure comes to pick people for the Passenger. What she tells them is all a lie.

The Doctor finds out the Division used Angels to do their dirty work.

Back in the basement the Doctor reversed the polarity of the neutron flow. Hoorah!

The girl sees an old woman in 1967. It's her aged 70 something.

The Doctor wants the Angels to get the rogue angel out of Claire, but the Angels want the Doctor. The Division want the Doctor and 'she is recalled to Division.' The Doctor turns into an angel.

Oh, and there is a mid-end-credits Vinder and Bel thing and no end music – because the Doctor is now an angel.

Mini Review

This is another story that should be quite strong with a good setting and good performances but marred by the need to tell the bigger picture. The whole story turns out to be ultimately pointless and just a way to have the cliffhanger. Don't believe me? OK, so this story is about the Angels wanting to get a rogue Angel back into the fold but then we find out the Angels worked for the Division and actually this is about getting the Doctor to work for the Division again. All the rest is cheap Angel scares which, let's be honest, have been done to death already (can someone tell me how stone creatures can rattle locks on doors and ring doorbells?) It did look good however, but so many threads are left undone they'll either be completely forgotten about next week or will be resolved preventing this from being the stand alone it says it is.

The Angels are inconsistent in their weaponry and the companions are underused and the Doctor is a bit unDoctory at times.

Survivors of the Flux

The Doctor isn't a statue very long and shouts at the Angels.

Dan and Yaz are living in real time, in 1904 in Mexico with Hugo Lang (sorry Jericho). Then they're in Turkey and a bomb goes off. Next, they're on a liner and they are attacked by a hood disguised as a waiter, with a serpent tattoo. Oh, and after three-years, Jericho is still calling Yaz 'Miss Khan.'

The Doctor is with an Ood (costumes still in stock?) and she meets the woman from two episodes before. She is from Division. They are outside the universe and the old universe is ending because of the Flux event and they're preparing to move to a new one. Division blames the Doctor because she escaped. They engineered the Flux, 'because they are scared of me' in the Doctor's words. The woman is the woman who found the Doctor: Techteun. And the ultimate apex of the universe destruction is you've guessed it – Earth.

Another curveball and it's 1958 and there's the Grand Serpent from Vinder's dreams because everything revolves around Earth. He's up to something. Then, it's 1967 the Grand Serpent is still in the secret service and the start of UNIT. The Tardis is in the office, found there from the Angel village in the previous episode. Then in 1987, the Grand Serpent retires.

Yaz has a Doctor hologram, and she watches the Doctor explain stuff. She clearly watches it to reassure her. She gives Yaz the mission to find the end of the world date.

The Doctor is given a pocket watch containing all her suppressed memories.

Present day, and the Serpent gets a dressing down from Kate Stewart about UNIT which he thinks should be shut down. Does this correct the terrible disbanding UNIT idea from *Resolution*, or was it seeded early. You can guess what I think…

Yaz et al go to Nepal which a bit of CGI makes Wales look like it. They didn't need that in 1967 when Wales last represented the Himalayas (*The Abominable Snowmen*). "Fetch your dog," says the wise man. That means, "Get Karvanista" - who doesn't have time travel.

The Great Wall is Cardiff castle btw.

And then the tunnels bloke appears, so they go to Liverpool to go in the tunnels

Vinder is swallowed by the Passenger and meets Di, who has scores to settle and seems to be some kind of warrior now.

The Sontarans are back via the Grand Serpent and Swarm and Azure are killing Techteun.

And why is Nicholas Courtney given a Lethbridge Stewart credit, did I miss a flashback, oh it was the voice over.

Mini Review

This is a funny one. On paper it works very well. You have some cute history bits with Yaz, Dan and Jericho, although it's a bit of a mess if you think about it for more than a second and all completely pointless filler. You have Vinder being put into position and meeting Di, who has sat in a weird Passenger world for a long time. You have Division being explained and killed off after all the build-up. You have the Grand Serpent being all suspicious throughout the UNIT era only to be a pawn in the bloody Sontarans' game again. In a universe as big as this what are the chances of Vinder, who worked for the Grand Serpent and the Grand Serpent both being pivotal to the story? Oh, and the tunnels are explained without really explaining them.

Therefore, it's a good example of the late period Chibnall Who storytelling, where interesting things are sacrificed for a less interesting whole and Earth is the centre of the universe. There is no peril, the threat is too CGI and the whole universe destruction is hardly going to get you cowering behind the sofa.

It's OK to watch, but really?

The Vanquishers

Sontarans are killed too easily, the fam go down tunnels to find an escape route. The Doctor is in three places at once. The Doctor gets a random explanation for the tunnels which doesn't really do it for me. The Sontarans are going to corner shops gorging on chocolate. Dear god. They are playing for allegiance.

Back in 1967 they go to save Claire because they need her. The Doctor has some scenes with Karvanista, which implies she was bad when they both worked in Division. Luckily for us Karvanista has something in his brain that means he'll die if he talks about it.

Vinder and Diane are in the Passenger and Diane has proper changed. It doesn't feel right, but there we go.

Can I say by the way I love the Sontaran ships. Oh, I have already. The Grand Serpent interrogates the Doctor. She can't die, script writers, you've blown that already. Whittaker is very good here but then it is ruined by the excessive need for jocularity. When the Doctor is got out of trouble by, um the Doctor, the jumping the shark factor has been cranked up to eleven.

The Doctor is baffled by Sontarans teaming up with other Who baddies.

Claire works out the new flux nexus. Well done, Claire.

The Passenger ravages. Vinder has managed to get out of it.

They send the tunnel guy back to his time zone; his plot contrivance is done.

The Doctor gets Vinder and Di.

The Sontarans are planning to use the other armies to absorb the flux energy. Save the universe and claim it as your own.

Jericho becomes the nice person who dies in any Chibnall episode and can't be saved because of technobabble.

The Sontarans speak of their plan now the Doctor has explained it.

The Daleks and Cybermen get zapped by the flux. The Doctor's friends do some technobabble.

The Passenger form can absorb the rest, which is also convenient.

Back on Atropos Swarm and Azure are killed off by Time itself. The Doctor gets the fob watch with her memories and now Time looks like the Doctor. Time tells her that her time is nearly ended. And hints that the Master ain't done because that's what Time does, it provides spoilers.

Vinder gets his revenge on the Grand Serpent and exiles him.

Di doesn't want Dan anymore, the universe is back to normal, but no explanation is given.

The Doctor apologises for going after Karvanista to find her memories and she sheds a tear. I think it's the first time the Doctor has wept. She hides the fob watch in the Tardis.

Look, it's childish, things get sorted out via words and waffle. Everything is reset as if it never happened, making the melodrama of the previous five weeks pointless. All the threats that overlayed each other are removed when the writer doesn't need them anymore. For example, Karvanista has lost his entire people, so he should be sad, but he's back to normal at the end. Or were the Lupari restored? No-one knows. Di is off with Dan but with no explanation as to how long she was stuck in the Passenger. Claire is back but there is no scene to reconcile the first time we meet her, and she has had the experiences. It's messy.

As depicted, a good chunk of our universe is destroyed and so are all the Sontarans, Daleks and Cybermen. Oh wait, but the next story is called *Eve of the Daleks*. You see, there is no consistency. Division is left hanging and we don't know whether we'll come back to it after Tecteun is killed. The Grand Serpent seems an elaborate villain to just hang around for the Sontarans. He is the highlight of the whole season but will probably never be seen again.

And even bigger, in the world of very right-on Doctor Who we have the Doctor casually exterminating three species and she doesn't even give it a thought. Genocide, where in the past the 4th Doctor didn't have the right (in *Genesis of the Daleks)* and what the 6th Doctor was accused of by the Timelords in *Terror of the Vervoids*. Inconsistent.

Why was Azure hiding out in the Arctic in the first episode? Why do the Ravagers hate the Doctor in particular? We know that Karvanista hates the Doctor because s/he let him down, but I bet we never find out how.

Much as everyone likes Vinder and he is well-portrayed, what is the purpose of the Bel and Vinder subplot? They could be completely removed, and it would make no difference at all.

The Doctor finds out she is from the next universe from ours (maybe). But she doesn't seem interested in visiting it. For a traveller this seems …strange.

And why, why, why after an entire season being dedicated to the Doctor trying to find out what happened in her past does she throw the fob watch of memories into a dark tunnel for the Tardis to keep from her?

Let's be honest there are too many unanswered questions and I suspect most of them will never be answered.

Overall Verdict:

This is tough to review. In some ways any criticisms of modern Doctor Who have been addressed by this already but nobody who is in the anti-camp is going to be moved by what they saw.

If you are going to study *Flux* as a piece of television or, even as part of the Doctor Who canon, the best place to start is with the release of the Chibnall/Whittaker explanation video on You Tube, so you can compare what they wanted to do and what we see.

Now, just re-read that again. The showrunner and the lead actor released a video on the official BBC channel to explain what we've seen. Take a moment, have you ever heard of such a thing, either in Doctor Who, or in any drama ever?

And when they explain it, there's a logical flow to the 'big picture' stuff. The universe bending, creating of the Time Lords, black ops stuff. But there is no sense that this was explained properly on screen.

Rewind. At the end of the last proper season that (remember) ended in early 2020 the Doctor was revealed to be more than a Time Lord and more of the genetic basis of the Time Lord race. Now, although it hurts to say it, that was a long time ago, and not that many people were watching anyway. Coupled with a global pandemic and you'd be right to assume that average viewers may not be fully up to speed with what happened.

As noted before, a simple 'Previously on Doctor Who' before the first episode would have been helpful here and would have helped people get up to speed with what happened in *The Timeless Children* 18-months earlier. That nobody thought to do that is a major error. And for all the positives on display here that first episode was criminally bad.

Therefore, you can see why *Flux*, filmed under tremendous stress in pandemic conditions, stinks to high heaven.

Even on re-watching in a block for this book, where, believe me it makes a hell of a lot more sense and the story is a lot easier to follow, it still never makes you do that edge of your seat stuff that Doctor Who was all about all those years ago. It's just there, being Doctor Who but tonally, all wrong.

Other famous reviews:

Anyone who could write all this does not understand Doctor Who at all. Not. At. All. So, all that? Gone. Never happened. Not in this universe. Nothing to see here – Androzani.com.

There is a sense of things being unfinished, of time being wasted, of opportunity squandered. For all its good qualities, it is hard not to view *Flux* as a breakneck scramble for the finish line, an ensemble of confused players rushing through the final act before the credits roll, yanked up at speed with the same indecipherable intensity as the drama that preceded them - Brainofmorbius.com.

The state of the universe seems to have been swept under the rug now that the story's over. Certainly, nobody's mourning the loss of trillions of lives out there, nor does the Doctor look like she's going to be trying to undo the damage given Yaz's cheerful declaration that they've "no idea" where they're going next. It's maddening to think that either Chris Chibnall has no intention of addressing the aftermath of his own creation, or that he does plan to but has mistakenly given us the impression that we shouldn't continue to care – Chris Allcock, Den Of Geek.

Ratings:

1) 5.81 million (9th)
2) 5.10 million (13th)
3) 4.67 million (20th)
4) 4.57 million (18th)
5) 4.83 million (21st)
6) 4.64 million (26th)

Ranking: 17/24

What have we discovered? That Doctor Who could work as a 10-part Netflix show but not this way.

Title: Eve of the Daleks

One Line Summary: Timey wimey stuff in 10-minute windows.

Written by: Chris Chibnall

Directed by: Anneta Laufer

She was never really a big Doctor Who fan "when I was a kid. I remember it being on TV, but I wasn't much into Sci Fi at the time." It is only when the reboot started that she took more notice. Some of her favourite specials from previous years include *The Runaway Bride, Voyage of the Damned* and *The Doctor, the Widow, and the Wardrobe.* More recently, she also really enjoyed *Resolution* and *Spyfall Part 1.*

Anything else before we start?

According to Chibnall it was written in a week, or two weeks, if you believe guest star Ashling Bea: this is confirmed from other sources. The read-through on Zoom was apparently hilarious and Adjani Salmon gave as good as he got with two professional comedians in the cast.

It was all filmed in Cardiff, despite the location being Manchester.

Laufer got contacted by producer Sheena Bucktowonsing, who had seen some of her work online – in particular, a Sci Fi short film directed called *Afro Punk Girl.* She decided to join Doctor Who was because, "I knew such a genre bending, epic story telling format was going to be a huge and fun challenge for me to embark on. Plus, I was going to work with the first female Doctor in the history of Doctor Who!"

Time was the big problem. "We had a lot to shoot in a short space of time while also making sure it looked cinematic and exciting." The locations were also a challenge – especially the narrow corridors. Moving around with cast and crew and equipment, and Daleks and abide by all the strict COVID-19 rules in place, made it very challenging. Chibnall had suggested Aisling Bea which Laufer thought was a great idea. Laufer knew Salmon from his web series *Dreaming Whilst Black* so when his name was put name forward, she was excited.

The Episode

The elevator pitch for this episode was clearly 'Rom Com with Daleks' (credit the director, not me) but that works well for this.

Is this the story that takes place over the shortest period of time - about ten minutes with timey wimey licence? Beating Chibnall's *42*? A very COVID set up with two people in scenes. But, like *Midnight* in the Davies era, this feels right. We're in a storage facility in Manchester and there's some chemistry between the owner and a client called Jeff.

It's nine minutes to midnight as the Doctor resets the Tardis to remove flux debris. They're not on the promised beach, but a storage facility in Manchester.

A Dalek arrives, kills Nick and the Doctor encounters the body. Dan doesn't know what a Dalek is. They always make such efforts to put Doctor Who in our universe and then you have a companion that's never heard of them. Unlikely. Then Ashling Bea gets zapped. The Dalek zaps the Doctor and fam. That is a good cliff hanger.

The same scene plays out with added 'hmmm, this is weird.'

We get weird comedy from the weird stuff in the storage pods. Beef and beans. The Dalek is ahead and gets them even though they do different things.

3rd time

"We're stuck in a time loop with killer robots"

More exposition and they all hide in the unit. The Doctor says each loop is less time than the last one and they are going to die for strategic reasons.

4th time

This is a bit better than *Heaven Sent* but obviously lighter in tone. Ashling Bea's running is unconvincing. We learn the flux was 'last week.'

The Doctor finds something explosive.

Ashling and Nick have one of those Chibnall conversations in a break from the action and although it's a perfectly good example - um you have 6 minutes guys. The Dalek clarifies that the Daleks weren't all killed by the Flux, just the 'Dalek battle fleet,' which is still in the millions. That does put in the head the idea of the stay-at-home Daleks, who work in call centres and at power plants and garden centres, but that train of thought makes you go off into all sorts of weird places. Go down that path and you realise how badly realised all Doctor Who monster societies are

The Doctor is vulnerable again and doesn't have authority. The rules change and now Nick is vulnerable. Nick does the whole 'duck and two Daleks exterminate each other' thing, which is so lame.

As another loop comes round and time is really short Dan has a chance to talk to Yaz about what she feels for the Doctor and as we find out later, he goes and tells the Doctor. Priorities mate Then they get zapped.

And in the next round Dan again decided that Yaz's feelings are his priority and tells the Doctor.

It's all coming down to the final minute with a decoy penultimate loop.

We get pained Yaz looks at the Doctor as the time runs out.

The plan works and you get cute New Year fireworks.

And the train crane guy from *The Woman who Fell to Earth* catches it on his phone. I thought we were in Manchester?

The Doctor avoids issues and goes to find lost treasure.

The 'Coming Soon' has Sea Devils. Squeeeeee!!

Verdict:

I'll give show runner Chris Chibnall his due, he doesn't

shy away from challenges. His predecessor was the master of the Timey Wimey stories, and it would therefore be perceived as sensible to avoid them but, oh no, Chibnall attempts one for the New Year Special. Brave or foolish? On balance brave, but only just.

The basic idea: the Doctor, companions and two humans (a lock up owner - the excellent Ashling Bea and Nick, a customer, the also excellent Adjani Salmon) are stuck in an ever-decreasing time loop where they are continuously murdered by Daleks angry at the Doctor's actions in *Flux*. It's a fine idea that reminded me of video games where you lose a life and must start again. Here though we had the added cleverness of an ever-shortening time span for the action to happen and that the Daleks are clever enough to work out how the good guys are going to change the game each time. The dialogue was sparkling and witty and having someone of Bea's calibre here just made everything funnier. It's as if she raised the game for the whole production.

As an hour of simple television watching, it worked a treat, and this was one of the best episodes of Doctor Who for a good number of years. It was pared down and told a simple story. Doctor Who used to work because the production team couldn't do good special effects and had to use their imaginations to produce great tv. And here, with four (maybe) 5 actors and COVID restrictions, they had to adapt.

Yet don't look too hard, because the whole thing is a contrivance, with little plot logic to hold it together. The Dalek, with their new machine gun-style weapons and the new ways of discussing things were good, if a little stupid at times. "Daleks don't have (sneer) friends," isn't as good a line as they think it is. It must be said though that Daleks were (as ever) very good at missing their targets when it suited the plot and lethal at other times. For a change, the Doctor had to use her wits and what was around her (and a lock-up has a lot of stuff to use). People who make Doctor Who, it's not hard to do. Yes, the end explosion was ludicrous, the supporting character romance might be a bit unlikely, but we'll take it.

Which brings us to the Yaz revelation. First, it has certainly been trailed for a while but given that the last female companion was gay, and at least four of the previous companions have been dreamy about the Doctor it's hardly as ground-breaking as it may have been made out. My feeling is this means it's really, not going to end well, but at least we get Sea Devils at Easter.

After the confusion of *Flux,* a simple, stand alone with a neat script and iffy premise will do even if it is not one that you will ever watch again. It's a one-off.

Other famous reviews:

[It] succeeds as a contained piece, a 'locked room' thriller sagging only in the middle – Radio Times.

Where *Flux* was knotted and clenched [this] is clean and neatly conceived" – Evening Standard.

Brimming with fast-paced jokes, hilarious slapstick, and impeccable comic timing…this is the most gripping Doctor Who has been in years - The Independent.

Ratings: 4.39 million (25th)

Ranking: 3/24

What have we discovered? A new, rather brilliant way of telling a Doctor Who story.

Legend of the Sea Devils

One Line Summary: How many times will they try and fail to make the Sea Devils interesting?

Written by: Chris Chibnall, Ella Road

Road is considered to be one of Britain's up-and-coming playwriters. After completing her education with a BA in English from Oxford University and a MA in Drama from the Oxford School of Drama, she started her professional acting career. However, after two-years of chasing around for fulfilling roles, she decided she wanted to be in charge of her career and turned to writing. her first play *The Phlebotomist*. She was named Britain's most promising playwright by the *Daily Telegraph* in 2018.

Directed by: Haolu Wang

She is an MA Directing Fiction graduate of UK's National Film and Television School (NFTS). In her words her works "explore the characters' psychological and emotional journeys. She creates immersive, subjective narratives, often blurring the boundaries between reality and imagination. Her storytelling sensibility leans towards psychological suspense, sci-fi, and fantasy." This was her first mainstream tv after a few short film productions.

Anything else before we start?

On the Doctor/Yaz thing Ella Road said: "It's not a huge part of the episode," Road explained as she described her enjoyment of writing the scenes. "But I think it's good to be able to include these real relationship questions that people can relate to, outside the whole sci-fi aspect of the show. The question of whether or not to enjoy a relationship for what it is now, versus worrying about the future – that's a very universal thing." It also felt really special to be able to write a queer relationship in the series," Road continued. "As a queer person myself, it felt like I'd been handed the opportunity to explore something in a way that was quite subtle, actually, and quite delicate."

Chibnall wasn't sure if he would use them, but he wanted them to look like classic Sea Devils. The sets were gigantic.

The beach scenes were filmed on Sully Beach in Wales.

The Episode

What a title! What anticipation! Every legacy fan has a soft spot for the Sea Devils - it's the beauty of the mask. Although, of course, their every appearance since their first one has been a disaster. But Chris, we have faith. I mean, just because a monster by design has a wobbly head and no clear motivation except to be Silurians for an episode with the Royal Navy, means they lack a bit of filling in. But let's see.

China 1807 - based on the music and a caption. It's raining. A woman with a serious attitude arrives. She's after 'the statue,' which is a giant sea devil. The dry-stone wall behind the statue doesn't feel very Chinese to me, more Yorkshire Dales. The snarling bad guy acting is a little over done, as if they've gone for children's television performance mode. She attacks the statue, and a guy comes to tell her not to. He is slain by … a sea devil.

The Doctor and crew land on the same beach and are dressed ludicrously. The Doctor wears earrings and they're being pulled towards the sea, as do skimming stones. The Doctor calls it a geo-magnetic disturbance, which is interesting given neither the rocks nor the metal in her earrings are magnetic. Chibnall goes on about this being for intelligent 8-years olds, but they seem to think getting the science totally wrong is ok. It's these things that show me they really never got it. It would take one Google to sort it and there is no one involved with the production who even cares to get it right. Yet someone would have been getting the Chinese costumes exactly right. It's fluff.

The Sea Devil is shown rampaging through the village - in the past? It was raining just a minute ago and now it isn't. Somehow the crew manage to orchestrate a trap - wichh is not explained - see above, this clearly was cut to ribbons before broadcast. To the Sea Devil's credit it escapes easily and gets on a CGI ship that flies in to get him. 'That's impossible,' says the Doctor, which is ludicrous. I mean how many impossible things does the Doctor see every story? A flying ship is de rigueur surely? And then the Doctor drops the line, 'the sea devils have a ship,' and you see that somewhere there was an ironic joke, but it has clearly been lost between the page and the staging and it doesn't work at all.

The woman dressed as a pirate introduces herself as Madam Ching and the Doctor gets all excited, but Ching is quite an obscure historical character. Dan suddenly knows a lot about 19th century piracy, like Ryan suddenly knowing about acetylene and dissection. I'm not saying he shouldn't, it's just convenient.

Sea Devils think of humans as land crawlers. And we get the classic *Jaws'* style direction of an attack of a fisherman's boat by a giant monster; the music even mimics it, which is cool but shows how little imagination is at work.

Dan pals up with the son of a killed villager (Ying Ki) who wants a piece of Madam Ching. They swim onto the ship undetected. There are no crew, for COVID reasons? For some reason Ying Ki thinks Dan is 70 and he splutters he's 42. John bishop is 56, which nicely, is halfway between the two. Ching finds them and somehow ties them up upside down on her own. That's ludicrous. Two men one of whom wants to kill her end up like that!? Dan then questions how she needs three people, yet she managed to tie him up alone!

The Doctor and Yaz go back in time to trace some treasure for Madam Ching, for no real reason. In 1533 Sea Devils coincidentally are also involved. The pirate is forcing his crew off the ship. Back in the 19th century they go to the wreck on the bottom of the sea. No issues with that but compared to *Logopolis* of course, oh dear.

"No ship Sherlock" oh dear (again) and then the big monster that's not a Myrka grabs the Tardis. There is a whole world down there and the Doctor does her wow thing and there are little lamp shades lit with presumably 21st century light bulbs. Nice of the Sea Devils to hand their tech over to land crawlers for us to use later! There's a key stone thing.

Madame Ching has a sad moment during the action, like was always get.

The Doctor makes the ship reach the surface and pirate Ji Hun is revitalised. There's some tosh about the Plutonic Crystals and flooding the land.

There's a swashbuckling sword fight and the Doctor does a somersault.

Ji-Hun and the Doctor kill the Sea Devil is annoyed.

Then as ever while saving the world Yaz gets a chance to see if Dan has talked to the Doctor about 'you know what.'

The Doctor quips about being not a bad date and then let's Yaz down a bit jokily. The 'can't' excuse. The Doctor can't fix herself. You know the usual rejection lines. 'Can we just live in the present?'

The usual minor character sacrifices himself. In this case Ji-Hun, who has to put two cables together. The Doctor seems happy for someone to offer to do the sacrificing and never even looks back! Oh dear.

And then the coming soon over the end credits has Ace and Tegan! Squeeeeee!

Verdict:

Before I start, we must mention the ratings. 2.2 million on Easter Sunday in the UK does not suggest the current incarnation of Doctor Who is 'must see' television. And quite frankly, it isn't. Like Capaldi's Doctor before her, the public has stopped watching and will wait for the new incarnation. This is not a criticism of Jodie Whittaker, nor Peter Capaldi, but it is a criticism of the programme they starred in and how easy it is to pander to fans rather than a general viewer.

Legend of the Sea Devils is simply shoddy. Yes, it looks great but, it's sloppy. Clearly it was designed as 1 hour special but had its time frame chopped. For example, the weird dialogue at the start about going to a beach but when they get out of the Tardis, they are clearly set for a pirate adventure is just ludicrous. There are other problems the usual twirl of technobabble to suddenly end the problem, which was only a technobabble threat in the first place. It's peril-free.

Then there's the Sea Devils. Created because there was the need for a Silurian sequel and the production team wanted to use the navy, they needed aquatic Silurians, Sea Devils sit in a strange position in Doctor Who fan lore. Big praise for the masks and the general idea, hilarity at the string vests and the general clumsiness. And the decision in *Warriors of the Deep* to make them grunts to the Silurian officer class sort of made sense, but pretty much ruined them. The modern ones look great (probably too cute) but apart from a bit of 2-second outrage from the

Doctor when the unnamed Sea Devil leader was killed there is none of the moral subtlety attempted 50-years ago. The lead (unnamed in the show) Sea Devil speaks like a generic bad guy and is even played by an actor who played a baddie last season. This is thin stuff.

There's some guff about pirate ships and is that sea creature supposed to be a super Myrka, or do the Sea Devils have other monsters we never see except in their stories? The resolution is resolved. The regulars do their thing well, but it just doesn't mean anything.

And the other big hit of the Whittaker era, the celebrity historical figure falls flat on its face here with a real Chinese pirate appearing: including Madam Ching. My knowledge of 19th century pirates was limited pre-broadcast and so to find out what an extraordinary person she was and how many ships she commanded was quite a shock. But here she is reduced to a sassy Disney princess action figure, which is a shame. The other one is just there to pirate the other ship. But Dan knows all about pirates and Ching, so that's ok.

Then, just at the end where the Doctor lets Yaz down gently we finally see a bit of old Doctor Who. Now, I have no opinion on the Yaz/Doctor romance speculation. I suspect it was an internet thing the production team ran with it, then a planned theme. But as ever it strikes me as weird that Yaz and the Doctor have spent quite a lot of time together in the Tardis (well nearly five years for us, at least a year for Yaz but this is a very conservative guess and that's ignoring the years in the past in *Flux*) and at no time has the Doctor mentioned she spent twelve-ish incarnations as a man? But that is the implication of the script at one point. Anyway, the whole thing is fluffy but the scene where Whitaker's hair is flying in her face as she explains to Yaz was the most Doctorish thing I'd seen in a long time, and it reminded me of how this show was always really about the power of ideas and words, rather than big spectacle.

This fails in so many ways. The plot holes and comic book manoeuvres, the use of magic as a real thing, the attempt at one-liners that aren't as funny as Steven Moffat's, despite having a professional comedian to deliver them. A lazy, idealess dragging up of old monsters then doing nothing interesting with them. An assumption that we'll watch because it's Doctor Who.

For me *Legend of the Sea Devils* was an absolute disaster, one of the worst stories ever made. And the regular viewers also agreed by not even bothering to watch.

Other famous reviews:

I struggled to care about this meandering story, which involved John Bishop looking as if he'd fallen on hard times and gone into panto in a pirate costume from Aldi. Carole Midgely – The Times.

A moody and oddly melancholic episode wrapped in the trappings of a grand pirate adventure it doesn't quite have the capacity to live up to - Den of Geek.

Sitting through *Legend of the Sea Devils* is like watching seaweed dry. The 50-minute Easter special has a problem in common with so much modern Doctor Who in that, while it abounds in action, CGI spectacle and bombastic music, there's a dearth of tension and suspense, there's no time for a slow build, no eeriness, no real appetite for proper frights or even the mildest stab at the macabre. Doctor Who can be, and is well-known for being, behind-the-sofa or edge-of-the-seat viewing but making that is almost a forgotten art - Radio Times.

Ratings: 3.47 million (almost certainly the least watched story ever)

Ranking: 24/24

What have we discovered?

Two times out of three appearances the Sea Devils are crap.

The Power of the Doctor

One Line Summary:

It's the end but this time it's really been planned for.

New Cast: Janet Fielding – Tegan

Born Janet Mahoney in Brisbane, she was a bit of a science geek at school but turned to acting at university. She moved to England in 1977. When Doctor Who was looking for an Australian air hostess, someone from her actors' collective wrote to then producer John Nathan-Turner saying they don't come any bossier than Janet. After leaving the show she became critical of it and became an agent, Paul McCann being one of her clients. She has softened her stance of late and is back doing Big Finish Audio plays. Although unrelated to this serious book I should confess that my first major adolescent crush was on Tegan Jovanka. I'm in good company though, so did *Full Circle* writer Andrew Smith, and he got to meet her (with obligatory knee tremble)

Sophie Aldred - Ace

Born in Blackheath, South London, she read drama at Manchester University. She then worked in fringe theatre and working men's clubs to get her Equity Card. She was in a production of *Fiddler on the Roof* when she got the call to audition for a part in Season 24's *Delta and the Bannermen*; she didn't get the part but made enough of an impression to get the part of Ace. It would be her first television work.

Post Doctor Who her career was less stellar, and she was a stalwart of the Big Finish audio adventures.

(Note, there are also hundreds of minor cameos, but you know about them.)

Written by: Chris Chibnall

Directed by: Jamie Magnus Stone

Anything else before we start?

This episode was a special request by the BBC for inclusion in their 100th birthday celebrations. Chibnall said the 'story was always going to end this way,' therefore the *Legend of Sea Devils* was made as an extra and the final story was bumped up to help the BBC. He also claimed that the Master, the Cybermen and Daleks being in it was always part of the plan, 'from way before we did *Flux*': take that any way you like. This extra episode meant that people's contracts had to be extended. The inclusion of Ace and Tegan was planned, Ace, because she was 'the most modern companion from that era' and Chibnall felt similar about Tegan. They were the only choices, so their availability had to be checked before writing began. Dhawan's availability had been checked during *The Timeless Children*.

The final moments were written early on because Chibnall knew what they were going to be for 'quite a while.' When pushed on this with the question 'years?' he replied 'Yeah.' On the final day Gill and Whittaker were applauded onto the set and Chibnall had never seen that happen before. Whittaker loved her final line. The final scenes were filmed in story order, for secretive reasons, the words written long before and put aside.

Although we knew Tennant was coming back, we fans didn't know anything more, nor did we know about the other Doctors, nor the companions. All leapt at the chance of coming back. Chibnall was quoted the following day as saying Tom Baker was asked but was unavailable. On set, Colin Baker called Whittaker 'the Boss.' Whittaker was incredibly nervous about meeting the old actors.

Chibnall was delighted by getting near centurion William Russell back for his cameo. The companions' therapy session was an emotional day and Whittaker came down, even though she wasn't in the scene.

The Episode

A space train is under attack from old-school Cybermen, but they seem strangely vulnerable. How the mighty have fallen. But it's just so they can be shown to regenerate into cybermasters, who are much more immune. The Doctor, Dan and Yaz are here to rescue a girl, and drop down onto the train in a very CGI way. The drops from Tardis to train look ludicrous. Explained by an 'electromagnetic roof' though why the roof would be an electromagnet is another matter. The Cybes are after 'the cargo.' Dan nearly gets shot and is saved by Yaz. The Cybes get their cargo/girl. They take her: good to start with a fail.

We cut to Siberia 1916 (big location naming is the Chibnall hallmark). It's one scene to say: RASPUTIN!

In London Ace (squee) is investigating missing paintings. She looks fab, if a little prosaic to be on Earth. Then she calls Tegan (squee!) she's investigating missing seismologists. She also been given a Russian doll from the Doctor in the shape of a Cyberman. It doesn't look like a Russian doll (they say Russian doll to hint at something, but no-one would look at that and say ooh it's a Russian doll. Action figure, yes). Shoddy work guys.

The Tardis is in Liverpool so Dan can go on a date, but actually he's off. That answers one of the questions about too many people (again). See ya Dan, you were harmless.

A Dalek image breaks into the Tardis claiming to offer the key to the destruction of the Daleks. First rule is never trust a Dalek, the Doctor knows this and effectively says so. We move on to following the girl trail to an extra moon in 1916. Ok.

Rasputin is the Master in St Petersburg. Much as I want to roll my eyes, it looks great. It's all pointless of course and as I've noted before it could all be done in the Home Counties in the present day. The second moon is 'volcanic life converted to metal on a planetary scale' and there is a second Tardis there, conveniently police box shaped. It's linked to the centre of the moon thing.

There's a 'rudimentary cloaking shield' hiding something. Why? The girl is there, and she is also linked but she is also a shield for underneath is a Qurunx, which is a huge energy conscience plot convenience thing that are exceedingly rare, and the Doctor has never seen one (remember that). The planet is the 'zenith of cyber conversion.' Cybermasters zap at them in the usual conveniently inaccurately way.

Then Kate Stewart calls the Doctor in to report missing seismologists and paintings. The Doctor meets Ace and Tegan. The Doctor looks startled, Tegan is suitably miffed and puts Yaz in her place. It's a great scene. The 'we used to be you line' is awesome. All the paintings have the Master's face on, and the Master invites them to a seismology conference 3.2k from Vesuvius. It'll be further from Vesuvius than that! It's a silly scene of shrunk seismologists. The Master tells the Doctor to leave, or it will be the day (she) dies, although he knows she won't go. Dhawan holds it together in his usual brilliant way, as he gets arrested.

Plot error 2: the Master is transferred in the Tardis. It's amazing how angry we get with the Master when he calls the Brigadier and idiot, goads Ace that the Doctor ditched her (kind of suggesting he reads the Virgin New Adventures books).

And now we add Vinder to the mix and he, by random chance, lands on the 1916 cyber planet looking for the missing Qurunx. So, the Doctor has never seen one, that's the Doctor, yet Vinder treats one as a normal thing. Dumb.

The Doctor lands in a Bolivian volcano to meet the rogue Dalek. There is a path in a volcano? Huh? She meets the rogue Dalek. Of course, it's a trap. Yaz sees the Daleks with a giant drill and really old fans love the *Dalek Invasion of Earth* vibe.

Tegan's cyber doll opens up and releases Ashad and loads of Cybermen. ASHAD DIED YOU IDIOTS! 'I killed him once, but he's forgiven me now,' says the Master, to cover the cock ups. Gold bullets don't work on them - phew. Ashad and the Master are the big hits from this era. There is a muscular brutality to Ashad that just works in screen, and as you will know I think Dhawan has been brilliant.

The Doctor is taken to 2016 to meet the Rasputin Master, who riffs on Eric Roberts' lines in the TV Movie (1996) and tries to call the story the Master's Dalek Plan, which again, is glorious. The Master wants to force regenerate the Doctor into himself. That will be three Masters running around. He will use the Qurunx to do it. And of course, he plays THAT Boney M hit and does the dancing. One suspects the research into Grigori Yefimovich Rasputin probably never got much further than this. But it's a good scene, nevertheless. And if I'm honest with you, the bit where the Cyberman and the Dalek turn to each other, as if to say, 'what?' is also glorious. The Master/Doctor gets straight into the Tardis and starts messing with her head. And he wants to ruin the Doctor's name forever.

Ace takes control and her jacket is in a convenient floor panel. (Squee, despite it being stupid). Her nitro and the baseball bat are also there. Ace and Tegan do stunts.

The Doctor/Master is wearing a McCoy uniform with a Tom Baker scarf and a Troughton recorder. Yaz steals the Tardis.

The Doctor is in a CGI world where she meets David Bradley playing the First Doctor (squee), then Colin (squee), and Davison (squee) and McCann (squee) and McCoy (squee) and of course it's glorious. All the actors get a good line, and the Doctor now knows there's a way out.

The Doctor pulls an AI hologram out of the hat that she transferred by static electricity earlier in the show, although apparently, she's been working on it for thousands of years. Vinder teams up with Yaz for about 5-minutes.

Tegan and Kate Stewart team up and Tegan gets another good line that riffs on air hostesses. Of course, she never did much air hostessing as we meet her before she starts work, but never mind. Ace jumps off the building but is saved by Yaz and the Tardis. She's going to stop the Daleks in Bolivia. Tegan gets her Fifth Doctor moment with the hologram. Closure and a Brave Heart Tegan. Then Ace gets her McCoy moment. Then she meets Bradley Walsh, and we have a lovely psychic paper scene. Although the slightly squirmy flirting between Bradley and Ace I could do without. It just seems wrong, but I can't work out why.

The volcanoes are erupted (from 1916) but in 2022. Jo Martin rocks up and freaks out the Master/ Doctor and the Cybermen do the 'shoot each other in a circle' thing. This is nearly another bad Chibnall trope. Vinder shoots the Doctor/Master. Chibnall remembers that Yaz hasn't met Jo Martin since she was still disguised as a tour guide in Gloucester. The regeneration is reversed.

Kate is being converted but Tegan, who fell off a ladder, but isn't hurt, rescues her. Ashad dies again. Daleks get zapped by nitro 9.

The Rasputin Master recovers.

All the gang work on the Tardis console. The Doctor fixes Vinder's ship (why is he in this?). The Doctor solves all the problems but gets zapped by the Master in the process to start the regeneration.

"Did she just turn exploding volcanoes into steel?" that's a line for the ages, given the composition of magma.

The dying Rasputin Master mortally wounds 13. The music gets serious, Yaz gets the Doctor. The Master escaped if you assume the CGI light moving away from the explosion is his escape.

Yaz takes everyone to Croydon off-screen. The Doctor starts to regenerate, and they have a last date on top of the Tardis. "I need more time." Yaz leaves, though why is a good question.

The Companions' Anonymous scene is glorious. William Russell at 97 is wonderful to see and Bonnie Langford and Katy Manning too (double triple squeee).

The Doctor goes to a CGI cliff like the one in *Broadchurch* (ha ha) "tag, you're it" and then she regenerates into David Tennant. Woah. I know these teeth

Oh, and What happened to the Master in 2022?

Verdict:

It will be years before we fully understand what was going on behind the scenes of Doctor Who in the Whittaker era. Chibnall started out with a clear direction of having absolutely nothing from the past of the show in the first season, even deliberately taking UNIT out of the equation and having the Doctor go to places where people have never heard of Earth. It was refreshing, if a little dull at times, but that dullness wasn't because of that decision.

One of the great weaknesses of Doctor Who fans is that we love the IDEA of old monsters coming back. A Classic Who Producer, who we won't name used to love the Squeee excitement when old, beloved enemies were announced as returning (only to give us *Warriors of the Deep*). It's hard to resist the pull of bringing back the old guard.

I'm ready to be proven wrong when the definitive history is told, but as noted earlier in the book, the huge change between Chibnall's first two seasons doesn't feel like the original plan. It feels like there was direction from above and if the Big Cheeses listened to complaints, it would have always sounded like 'BRING BACK OLD MONSTERS!' Whatever the truth is, we end up with this: the most BRING BACK OLD MONSTERS episode ever.

It's almost impossible to know where to start, except to say, it was very enjoyable. How can it not be to see the brilliant Sacha Dhawan playing the Master playing Rasputin? However, it's never exactly clear why he's doing it, or why he needs to be in St Petersburg in 1916.

But the surprises also keep it interesting. It started with a typically irritating and cartoony pre-credits sequence where the Doctor and companions defy the laws of physics and run around a space train shouting. This is a very Chibnally sequence of too childish, too much technobabble, over CGI'd action, which doesn't do what it needs to do. (A note on the CGI, it wouldn't surprise me if *everything* we see wasn't filmed in a small room in front of a green screen. It's looks like a computer game.

Then of course we get the return of Ace and Tegan. No Doctor Who fan is ever going to moan about them returning. Both seem to be working on mysteries that involve the Master's face on old Masterpieces (why?) and seismologists. Both Sophie Aldred and Janet Fielding give it a good go, Aldred perhaps more convincing as an acting performance, Fielding perhaps more convincing as a spurned ex-companion. I can't imagine Ace is on Earth. It just doesn't compute. The Virgin New Adventures are canon, surely?

Anyway…the big worry for me before watching was what are they going to do with so many characters (don't forget Kate Stewart too)? This was answered pretty early when Dan decides he's off. Good decision, but then they bring back Bradley Walsh at the end. Why? Then Vinder shows up and is given precisely nothing to do. Even the Doctor seems surprised to see him.

The Master's three-pronged Dalek, Cyberman attack is gloriously pointless, as is his forced regeneration of Thirteen into him (further confounding the pub quiz question 'How many Doctors are there?). The cameos by the classic Doctors via the hologram are nice of course and we always like to see them.

It all plays out in the usual way, technobabble and explaining loudly. The Doctor somehow wins and gets wounded but not enough to allow her a touching and quite sweet scene with Yaz. Quite why Yaz couldn't be there to see who the next version is weird, but there we go. Some have speculated that there was some off-screen agreement, but that sounds so weird. "When I regenerate you aren't going to be there to see it." – unlikely. And then THAT regeneration scene, well it was brilliant, as was the Companions' Anonymous scene, but I would have liked to have seen Polly and Dodo too (joke).

Finally, the ratings – poor, as we know and as this was followed by the Old Production team getting back together and giving out spoilers and revealing new companions on Telethons you realise that all the secrecy took Doctor Who out of the limelight. When it was off air for over a year between *Resolution* and *Spyfall* momentum was lost. That approach failed Doctor Who and left it in a precarious position.

Overall, it doesn't know this, but it was a perfect summary of the Chibnall era: it caught us out, it looked gorgeous, but it made no sense at all.

Other famous reviews:

It is by no means the weakest script Chibnall has given us, but neither is it the strongest…but Whittaker manages to rise above the noise – Den of Geek.

I loved Whittaker being the Doctor; I just wish I could have loved being with her a bit more, too – Isobel Lewis, The Independent.

[It] may not have been the perfect ending but it's still a fitting tribute to a great Doctor- Evening Standard.

"It's probably a good time for [Whittaker] to go, because her mode of slightly pop-eyed positivity – insisting that, despite Daleks, Cybermen and the Master trying to destroy the world, everything will be fine – is now disturbingly reminiscent of a Liz Truss speech – Private Eye.

Ratings: 3.71 million (4th)

Ranking: 7/24

What have we discovered? Wasted opportunities.

www.ingramcontent.com/pod-product-compliance
Lightning Source LLC
Chambersburg PA
CBHW051553250726
48653CB00004BA/1123